In The Beginning
There Was Physics

togul

In The Beginning
There Was Physics

Frank Kuppner

Polygon

© Frank Kuppner, 1999

Polygon
22 George Square, Edinburgh

Typeset in Meridian
by Hewer Text Ltd, Edinburgh, and
printed and bound in Great Britain by
Bell & Bain Ltd, Glasgow

A CIP record for this book is available
from the British Library

ISBN 0 7486 6248 0 (paperback)

The Publisher acknowledges subsidy from

THE SCOTTISH ARTS COUNCIL

towards the publication of this volume.

Contents

A Dreadful Miscalculation

E ager to try out the effect for ourselves, to see whether or not this thing we had heard so much about from well-informed close friends would really happen, when we managed to reach the top we scouted the upper slopes of the ben for a suitable target or specimen. When at last we saw a rock which was large enough for our purposes and at the same time looked sufficiently rounded and freeable, we hurried over to it, laughing and joking. Once there, joyfully, we pushed at it with all our combined might, and we were eventually rewarded, after considerable and sustained endeavours, with the sight of it first trundling away from us, and then beginning to hurtle off down the mountain, gathering further momentum at every second of its intensifying flight. Fortunately, it stayed on the ground all the way.

Having achieved this initial triumph, we laughed, kissed and congratulated each other, but then, although profoundly excited, we solemnly refrained from further self-indulgence and hurried back down to the parked car. It was so cunningly placed that this did not take us long. We drove back to town as quickly as we could. The traffic was fairly light, and we made good time. When we eventually came round into our own street at some speed, we drove up in front of the house, not bothering to put the car into the garage in order not to squander a single precious second of the advantage we supposed we had gained. Then we ran down the pathway to the door at the side. We were both quite confident. In fact, to be quite honest, we were both extremely confident. The result seemed to be, wholly and utterly, a foregone conclusion. The possibility of defeat never so much as crossed our minds. After this, there would have to be children and success, and all that sort of thing generally.

And yet, there it was, waiting for us, when we got there all the same. The large rock stood waiting for us at our back door. One could almost fancy to oneself that it was smiling. That, however, would obviously have been absurd. Those sorts of thing don't smile. Yet, it was wholly mystifying to us how it could possibly have travelled such a considerable distance in such a brief interval. Somehow, by a means wholly unknown to us, it had managed in its swift progress to skirt various arms of the sea, which cannot have been at all easy to interpret properly unless one was able to read roadsigns – not to mention various bridges, lights, unforgiving corners, unfortunate gradients and so forth. Could it possibly also have paid its way through the toll? All in all it was a considerable puzzle. Particularly to us, who had formerly been so confident.

We went into the house, subdued, to see if we could have a bit of a talk about it. It was important to try to be mature. It was not a useless episode. Some progress was made as we confronted the harsh issues. Nonetheless, when we came back out, an hour or so later, it was still there. I think I may honestly say it still is, although it is a while since I have remembered to look. We had our plans for it; we were always going to do something with it. But the fact is, for all our idle talk on this morning and on that evening, it is still there, pretty well exactly the same as it has always been. Needless to say, we have no intention of going back to the ben, or to any one similar, or of trying anything like that again. Once is enough. Also (and this thought occurs to me more or less every day) we are extremely fortunate in having a quite separate second door to our house as well, the door at the front. There are plenty of people who don't have our opportunities. That is certainly something we should try never to forget. We are thus able to ignore it completely for long stretches of time. That helps, I suppose. It is not perfect, far from it; but it does help.

A Bit of a Mystery

With a straight face I pocketed my winnings, and soon afterwards I was out in the street below in the pleasant chill of the morning, walking home, laughing to myself as I wondered when if ever they would realise just what it was they were invariably doing wrong. It was so easy. I could have taken a taxi, of course; but the coolness and the new quietness were such attractive contrasts to the overheated noisy house I had just left. Besides which, I did not live too far away. It was a perfectly reasonable thing to do, to walk carelessly back home, savouring a no doubt well-merited, but still pleasingly luck-blessed triumph. Long may they continue!

As I was turning the corner by the Gardens, I saw one of those little itinerant nocturnal cafes, those food kiosks or refreshment vans which come out of hiding and settle in various parts of the city during the dark – so that those who work at night, or those who are simply passing by, can stop for a chat or for a snack or for the inauguration of what turns out to be a lasting or transient acquaintance. I had not eaten for several hours, since I find it can interfere with my play. When the stakes are high, or the opposition is unduly keyed up and is clearly looking to try something on, it is a risk just not worth taking. Nor, obviously, does one drink anything stronger than water under those circumstances or any like them. However, catching sight of the kiosk, I thought I would quite like to celebrate with a modest beef sandwich or some such delicacy, and I crossed the broad, quiet road, making my way towards the bulky trailer, which, as it were, had its back to me as I approached. I think I already felt that something a bit strange was happening.

When I reached it and made my way round to the service counter, I saw that the place was entirely deserted. There were no takers on the pavement, and no-one was visible in the brightly lit but cramped interior at the back of the van. I called out to attract some attention, though I thought this might be a pretty forlorn hope. 'Yes? What is it?' said a woman's voice immediately from somewhere up nearer the front of the vehicle, a surprisingly quiet and distinct sound to emerge so suddenly from such an unbroken silence. I wondered for a moment where else voices might be hidden, very close but still out of sight. I thought a ham and egg roll might be just the thing, so I put in a modest, tentative request for one. Then I thought it over for a second or two, and changed the order, asking for a pair of them instead of just the single. 'Two ham and egg rolls it is then,' said the apparently disembodied voice.

What next? Something absolutely incredible happened next. However, without wishing to be too tantalising, I think it would be better for me not to say anything about it after all, for I am quite sure that virtually no-one would believe me. Well, they might or they might not, but I would rather not take the risk. I do make things up sometimes, of course I do – very often, in fact – but I wouldn't be making this up; and yet I suppose people would inevitably think that that was exactly what I was doing. So, if you don't mind, I think I'd rather just not bother. My view is that you are better not confusing reality and fantasy. I decline to put myself in such a needlessly false position, that is all. Let us just suppose that in fact nothing else happened, and that I walked home a minute or two later and soon afterwards clambered, still joyful and untroubled, into my weary and welcoming bed. Why not? That gets over the difficulty easily enough. Good.

A Death

There was once a young psychologist or store-detective called Lee, who went to the great local pleasure lake with a friend of his, named Erh, for it was the great holiday of the Fifth, and the whole day was theirs to spend as they wished, within reason. One of them was also a thief. One usually is. There were many people already there, including not a few adulterers, who had come out from the nearby town at an even earlier time, and the lake was much traversed with pleasure craft of various shapes and sizes, several of them clearly not meeting the requisite safety standards obtaining in that *fu*. At times shouts were heard. Nonetheless there remained further vessels waiting for hire, and the two friends engaged one of the smaller craft, and then began to gaily row out towards one of the many islands, whether natural or artificial, that dotted the broad surface of the water. It may safely be guessed that not a single person there was discussing the likely sexual identity either of the latest pope or of the newest prominent leader of Chinese Muslims. For that at least we should I suppose be grateful. Eee.

The hours passed slowly, in delirious happiness. They

were able to buy or steal refreshments from numerous of the little kiosks that were strategically situated at scrumptious points on the shore-line, or on the larger islands. There were even a few floating restaurants from which replenishments could be freely got. Numerous obscenities took place. Unfortunately, Erh fell overboard or otherwise escaped into the fairly shallow water at around three or four in the afternoon, and he was never seen again; but that was the only detail of Li's day which did not go entirely to plan. Asia, eh?

It was almost dark, and the lake was noticeably less busily plied than before, when the two decided to return the craft to the stage where they had engaged it, buy something warm to eat, and return to the nearby city before the day had entirely gone. They sat in silence, each thinking eagerly about prostitutes. When they finally managed to locate the required place, all around lay in total silence. They tied their boat to one of the staves at the edge of the sheltered pool among the trees of the little commercial inlet, and then made their way out of the enclosed park towards the main road. They passed no-one at all as they did so. They began to suspect that something had recently happened that they knew absolutely nothing about. The nearby city was no longer there either, which greatly puzzled them. That was definitely a surprise. In fact, the whole thing was difficult to understand. They could hear traffic off in the distance somewhere, but none of it ever quite reached the road they had set off down. This is the last time I'll ever do something so terrible to anyone, said one to the other; but the other did not reply. He looked, frankly, unconvinced. Who can blame him? After all, very often words are cruelly cheap.

A Lesson For Us All

Abraham, the ancient father, the beloved of God, the friend of the Deity, the man of worth and value and of all that is good in the spirit, sighed yet again as he lifted his sharp, keen member up into the air. Oh, I very much beg your pardon: that should be, his sharp, keen *blade*. After all, it is not a question of symbolism, is it? In another couple of seconds, his innocent young son Godron would be dead, stuck and slaughtered, killed by that righteous blade, and by that noble, kind, wise, learned, compassionate hand. The Lord had asked Abraham to sacrifice his son, and it was not for the slave of the Lord to attempt to bandy words with his Deity. If the Lord wanted his son's life, the Lord must be given it. Where was the difficulty? Had the Lord asked him to sodomise his son, or had He commanded him to allow himself to be buggered by his son, he would joyously have submitted to these requests of the Lord too, though normally nothing would have been further from his mind. It was, above all, a question of humility. He was the Lord's particular friend; and therefore it was his particular duty to be humble. No matter what the Lord might ask for, he obviously must have his reasons for doing so – good reasons, even if they were not for Abraham, as a mere mortal, to understand.

The Lord, however, would surely never request from one of his servants any act even remotely so disgusting as that. One would have to be raving mad to believe otherwise. Only someone already inclined to pederasty would surely hear the Lord – or rather, *imagine* he heard the Lord – make such shameless demands of him. Even in hearing messages from the beyond – perhaps particularly then – one had to be careful to cling to one's sense of proportion. But enough of that. No room for indecision here. Abraham raised his right arm high into the air and paused briefly to offer the appropriate prayer. The right was of course the proper arm for a sacrifice; using the other arm would turn it all into a farce, a sick joke, a betrayal of the lawfully and awfully constituted ceremony. It would have no virtue at all. Not that the other hand did not have its own fixed purpose too. It was for holding the boy's face, shoving it irresistibly backwards so that the neck was fully exposed, ready for the pious incision.

And then, just as he was about to plunge the blade into the appropriate place, for the greater glory of God, as demanded by God himself – a puzzling combination of circumstances, certainly, for the limited human mind – lo, out of somewhere, or out of not quite somewhere, an angel materialised, whatever that is exactly. Someone with wings anyway. Whatever it is it must have a physical component, for the angel tugged sharply at Abraham's right wrist, and the action caused the blade to loosen and plummet out of his grasp. See, for instance, if you don't believe me, the picture by Rembrandt, dating from 1635, now I believe in the Hermitage in Saint Petersburg. Who is going to get the details of such an event right, if not Rembrandt? He was, after all, more or less there at the time, I suppose. His is, obviously, the confidence of the eye-witness. Doubtless many people by now had stood in front of it and said 'F–!' – although most often, I dare say, in Russian.

'Stay!' said the Angel. 'Stay. This is no longer necessary. Perhaps it never was. Can you truly think that the Lord Your God requires the fulfilment of so obviously symbolic an act? Oh, ye of little faith! It is not so. Why should he want more blood? Do you think he is short of it? But he is short of nothing. He has an entire ocean of blood up there as it is – and a bigger ocean than anything the Earth can boast of, believe you me. Why should he want another small bodyful? Even now, He looks down on you from Heaven, smiling at your obedience. Look up! Look up! Can you not see him? Try to be careful where you look too. Look. Up there! Can you not see his wonderful, imaginary grin?'

And so, still exquisitely obedient, Abraham looked up, but he was able to see only clouds and parts of trees. He was a little confused. Then, startled by a change in the angel's expression, he looked down to the body of his son. What he saw caused him to loosen his grip on the juvenile's face. For what had happened was this. The knife, plunging (generally speaking) towards earth, had instead fallen deep into the child's body somewhere about the midriff, and the life's blood had already substantially poured out over him and dripped down onto the grass. He inspected the boy's eyes, and saw that they were already glazed and expressionless. If not dead already, he would be so within a few moments. Abraham turned his gaze back to Heaven and cried out joyfully, 'Thy will be done! Thy will be done! How could I ever have hoped for greater respect and compassion from Heaven than this?'

And from heaven there instantly descended a voice which said, 'Of course My will shall be done. How could

13

anything else possibly be the case?' And the angel murmured, 'Tragic. Unanswerable. Tragic. You ought to have tried to be a bit more careful, really. There's no point trying to shove the blame off on someone else.' And then he briskly disappeared, leaving Abraham to bury the body by himself, which he did almost at once, with two or three profound emotions in his heart. Hardly surprising really, given the circumstances. Still quite nice weather today, isn't it? Yes, indeed. We all have so much to be grateful for.

Hitherto Unrevealed Details

A t their wits' end in their attempts to solve the brutal murder of the young girl, the police even had recourse to a celebrated psychic from Greater Luxemburg who had repeatedly written to them, claiming vast previous experience in this field. His demands were modest and to the point. He claimed that if they would only fly him over to Glasgow and put him up in a half-decent hotel near the scene of the crime, he would be quite willing to spend a few days wandering around the area sniffing for clues, until an answer to the appalling mystery mystically coalesced within his primed mind. What could they lose? With a sigh, having just read heated, fearless calls for his resignation from the leading papers for at least the third time that month, the Chief Inspector picked up a phone and ordered a subordinate to make the necessary arrangements, if possible by a route which was not unbearably direct.

Three weeks later, there was a news conference arranged in the Function Suite of a major city-centre hotel by the popular tabloid, the *Daily Underpantselastictwanger*, which had agreed to meet all costs in return for being first with the story of all significant developments. After many days of intense scrutiny, invariably with a posse of journalists in tow, Monsieur August Petroozers was at last willing and able to reveal to the world what he had discovered. It was, naturally enough, given at the most suitable time of day for the forewarned *Underpantselastictwanger* to be sure that it would be able to capitalise on Monsieur Petroozers' revelations, and that its rivals would be subjected to the maximum logistical inconvenience in their attempts to follow the story. The first copies of the relevant edition were hitting the streets even as he spoke.

Monsieur Petroozers was very soon introduced to the alerted multitudes. He coughed and blinked. Then he looked up at the assembled news-gatherers and began to announce his measured findings in a thin but confident voice.

'The man who committed this murder will certainly kill again,' he said firmly, 'unless he is caught. Have no doubt of that. I have at last made contact with his aura. It was a hard aura to catch. It was fiendish. It was malign. It tried to evade me. It tried. God knows it tried. It was, as you say, tricky. Most fiendish of all, it knows a way of getting into expensive cars and escaping just when I am approaching. That is the sole reason why it took me three weeks to learn as much as I now do. Allow me to proceed at once to my discoveries. Questions in the right spirit may be asked afterwards, after my discussion, of course. Perdoing.'

In the seat next but one to Petroozers, the Deputy Chief Inspector pursed his lips in a gesture which was interpreted in a wide variety of ways, few of them, to be honest, registering any very favourable verdict on the present course of proceedings. He looked up as a minion came over to him, handed him a document, and lowered his head to speak confidentially into the ear of his colleague.

Petroozers did not notice this. 'What have I learned?' he continued unconcernedly. 'Let me tell you. I shall tell you all. I shall keep nothing back. Anything which I omit, through sheer inadvertence, this may freely be read later and in whole in the already current edition of the *Underpantselastictwanger* – for such are the miracles of modern technology. But it is not of those that I have to speak. And crumbles.

'Know then, that I see a man with dark hair. Yes. Darkish hair. He is in his late twenties. Yes. Twenty-three perhaps. Or is that thirty-two? The numbers can play little tricks, you know. He has been involved in crime before. Oh, he has just sworn! He has cursed. He must realise that I am getting near to him. Yes! He is of average height, or slightly smaller. He can look at times taller. We must take care. Yes. He has immensely strong heterosexual impulses, which from time to time overpower him. He is, in short, a raving pervert. His surname, I am quite sure, begins with an R or perhaps an M. These letters always tend to lie so close together. The word Donald, or something like it, is also in there somewhere I think. Yes. Ah! He goes! Yes. The rest, most unfortunately, remains hazy even now, because of immature imbrications in his image-plasma. He is that sort of type. It is, however, certain that he lives near comparatively near to the scene of the crime. His ability to form long-term relationships is, er – what?'

At this point, to no small initial irritation, the Deputy Chief Inspector intervened in an ostensibly apologetic manner, which was nonetheless observably suffused by a certain deep if restrained contentment.

'Gentlemen,' he said deferentially. 'Ladies and Gentlemen. I'm afraid I am going to have to leave you now to check a report I have just had in from New Zealand. It

17

could be the lead we were waiting for. In fact, if the details are as they have just been presented to me, it is hard to see how it could be anything else. If you'll kindly excuse me.'

He rose to leave. Everywhere there was a muted and baffled consternation. Was this the answer? How had authority come by it? Joyfully, Petroozers cried out that his honour had once again been vindicated, despite all the doubters. 'No sooner have I', he cried, 'been introduced to a case, than it cracks open like a shell or private part of some kind, helpless before my mighty thrusting aura. Dwunger! It is forever the same. I claim no great personal credit for it.'

Insistently pressed as he was by the crime reporters then present for a fuller statement, the Deputy Chief Inspector appeared to hesitate for a moment. Only when Petroozers begged him not to fail him now and go back on his word, the word which he had so solemnly given him, and a word which actually he had not the slightest recollection of ever having given, did he return to the heart of the hall which he was just about to leave, and routinely deliver himself of the following terse but highly amplificatory and informative speech.

'Oh, very well. I think it ought to be safe to share this with you now. The truth about this very sad affair is as follows, if documents now in our possession are to be believed – and I see no reason to doubt them. Apparently a naturally blonde grandmother in her late seventies, a strikingly tall and good-looking lesbian of hitherto blame-less character, has just killed herself in Dunedin. As you doubtless all know, that is in the South Island of New Zealand. I cannot possibly give you her name yet. Who can blame her indeed – particularly given that she has left a suicide note which confesses to the perpetration of this foul crime in a bout of temporary insanity which she has only recently become fully aware of, and which she found it impossible to live with the ever-growing knowledge of. I think I can risk telling you, however, that her surname begins with an N –'

'Which is virtually what I myself predicted!' cried Petroozers triumphantly. 'N and M are usually reckoned by professional seers to be more or less interchangeable. It is the same with U, V and W. It is a part of the most basic of our techniques.'

'A bag was found near her body,' placidly continued the Deputy Chief Inspector, 'which contains some items which were known to be missing from the dead girl's purse. The suicide note gives further details which were never revealed, and which would have been known only to the police and to the murderer. You may I think take it that the matter is as good as solved.'

'Triumph! They were of a sexual nature, these hitherto unrevealed details, were they not?' asked Petroozers.

'No,' replied the Deputy Chief Inspector. 'They often are, I agree; but this time they were not. I don't see how, in this case, anyone could reasonably think that.'

'Oh really? And who, my dear Inspector,' asked the great psychic, 'is to judge as to precisely what is sexual and what is not? This matter is not as trivial as you seem to think, quite apart from the notorious limitations of reasons, which is something I for one am very well placed to speak of. Particularly well placed, in fact. Is not, in the last resort, to a certain type of mind, absolutely everything sexual? Had you thought of that?'

'Possibly,' replied the Deputy Chief Inspector. 'Though I myself think not. And now, if you will excuse me. There are certain steps, formalities though they no doubt are, which yet require to be carried out before the case can be formally closed as solved.'

A growing murmur greeted these revelations from the Deputy Chief Inspector. The generally respectful atmosphere of the room towards Petroozers noticeably changed – all the more so after the departure of most of the police contingent. Petroozers shook his head sorrowfully. He could read the signs. It was all so sadly familiar. Nonetheless, he felt the desire to be, as best he could manage, in a generous, conciliatory mood.

'I fear,' he said, 'that in those details which do not correspond to what I myself saw with my own eyes, the confidence of the authorities will soon be proved to be sadly ill-founded. It is not a question of what we want. It is a question of what is. So many people in this sad world seem to find it so easy, my friends, to forget that.'

'Look!' called one of the exultant rival journalists, who was glorying mightily in the expensive discomfiture of the *Twanger*. 'The fact is you were almost completely wrong. We have taped it. What did you get right? The fact is that both you and the management of the *Daily Underpantse-lastictwanger* are left with egg all over their ectoplasmic faces. Is that not right? How is it wrong? "Comparatively near to the scene of the crime", you said? New Zealand? Comparative to what, for God's sake? The Andromeda Galaxy?'

At this a cry of anger escaped from an incensed Petroozers. 'Certainly not,' he cried. 'See! It is always the same! Already the true account of events is being scandalously rewritten. Already the forces of reaction and ignorance are seeking to throw dust on the true account of events – making out that nothing whatever that I said was right. They hate truth. They hate progress. They hate reality. They hate the forces that I represent. Donald and Dunedin – is it not virtually the same name? And as for the name itself, did I not say it began with an 'N'? Did I not say that with my own lips? I know perfectly well that I did. As do you, sir. Did I not mention New Zealand? Did I not hint at sexual peccadilloes? And already all this truth is being denied! It is always to make one, almost I mean, to abandon the patience and let them rot in future what! You know it as well as I do.'

'You know nothing!' shouted another of the motley crew. 'You say nothing! You simply recycle what you've managed to sniff out, and you combine it with the average this and the average that, so you can hardly fail. And this time it was not average at all, so you are left looking like the crook and charlatan you are! You're a fraud, sir! A gross fraud, if I may say so; just like more or less all the rest of them!'

'Charlatan, said he?!' cried Petroozers. 'Charlatan? I show you who is no such charlatan. Listen. Listen to this. I give you great and magnificent secret here. I wish to speak about the forthcoming end of the world. What of that? Eh? Wish you hear this or not?'

It is a truth universally acknowledged, that to claim to be able to speak with some authority about the forthcoming end of the world is usually a sure means of gaining the attention of one's wayward audience. This was no exception. The dissent of the crowd was instantly somewhat diluted by this bold stroke, and soon it began to trickle noisily away.

'What can you possibly know about the end of the world?' enquired one fashion writer, mildly interested. True, it wasn't fashion, but still – it wasn't *wholly* tedious either.

'I can tell you everything about it,' replied Petroozers. 'Everything. They do not wish to know, but I know, and I tell you. It is a terrible story. Too terrible for some.'

'What do you know? Tell us, August,' cried one of the

luminaries of the *Twanger*, only too glad to have this opportunity of wriggling free of the net of incipient farce within which his enterprise had been caught. 'Do you perhaps have some special information about it vouchsafed to you via your mystic powers?'

'Exactly that is what I have,' replied Petroozers. 'Exactly that. It is what exactly I have – information about that; about the impending end of the world. You are more right than you know, sir.'

'Then what is it for God's sake?' cried the voice of a newly exasperated rival. 'This could be vital, for the love of mercy. There could be a lot at stake here, you know. The whole world; our children; the timing of the cup final; the royal family itself – that sort of thing. Tell us. It is your duty as a concerned human being to tell us all you know about this.' Innumerable pens and recording machines were held up at the ready. What if there should indeed, despite appearances, be something in it? No-one, obviously, could take the risk of missing a story like this.

'I know,' replied August. 'I know this only too well. Who knows that more than myself? There is at stake here nothing less than the fate of the entire world. The whole world! I am aghast, genuinely aghast, at my own extreme vision. At the extent of it.'

'Oh, aren't we all? Now get on with it!' yelled an exasperated reporter – and her cry was taken up in various forms by so many people that August saw at once that further preamble would be counterproductive and that an immediate recourse to supporting statements would now be necessary. He was ready for this. All was as it should be.

'I shall not hesitate no more,' he said. 'Listen. Just listen.'

They listened.

'It is a known fact, which scientists are hiding from you, that a large meteorite – or asteroids, as they are sometimes called – is heading even as we speak at this very moment, it is heading towards the Earth. It is vast. It is larger than the big rock at Dumbarton by several times. Much larger, I think. It is horrible. It will kill us. It will crush us. It will end us and our lives on earth forever if we allow it to and if we do not attempt to stop it.'

Success. An utter silence had descended on the previously vibrant and noisy room. Of one mind his listeners waited for him to continue. Petroozers relaxed inwardly as he observed the difference his latest revelation had had on them.

'Indeed it is so,' he continued. 'It is indeed so. Even as we speak the meteoroid called Psionax after an extinct bird is hurtling towards the Earth at an unmentionable speed. Although Earth moves fast, it moves much faster. Look! Jets are nothing. It moves faster and us than we can hope to escape. But we cannot. Soon they must collide. Boof! If they do, it will be the end for everybody. Completely the end. Except perhaps for those whose thought waves are able to influence or to be technical bend the spore of the great trondler. We know this. Be aware of it. They will perhaps survive. They may be swept away to wherever nowhere is and be gone. They may even, think of this, be swept up onto Psionax itself, where their glory shall enable them to make a new life for themselves; a unique life; an admirable life. They will be welcomed in the Town Hall. Or they may remain here on the Earth, solely able to survive. That much is not clear. What is clear, however, is that most of us will go, almost all of us, unless we learn in time to channel our minds and their properties to the full. Do you wish to do this, my friends? Do you truly wish to do this?'

'Yes,' said three or four voices, low and intense among the silence of the shocked and bemused others.

'Good,' said Petroozers. 'That is good. Fortunately it is simple enough. I can explain how it is done. It is not difficult. It is in my book. This may be bought in shops. All who practise, and who do not slacken, may give out the right signals. And if enough learn to do so, and we have sufficient time, then we may yet save us all.'

'How much time have we got, Mr Petroozers, do you think?' asked the man from the *Daily Hole*.

'I say, about a month or two. Ten weeks at most, I think. But there may be error in the calculation. Perhaps twenty-five years at most. Who can be sure? The important thing is to take those steps and those steps only that—'

However, it so happened that at just this point there was the loud, entirely unexpected sound of shattering glass. Before anyone could quite make out what was happening, a small meteorite roughly the size of a woman's hand burst in through the nearby window at the side of the room. It flew through the air, and struck Petroozers on the head, killing him instantly. Then it fell to earth beside his inert and now cooling body. It had touched no-one else at all.

It was some moments before anyone began to understand what had just occurred. Soon some isolated screams and a buzz of renewed conversation enlivened the chastened room yet again. Almost always it is to some extent a tragedy to miss out on the scene of one's greatest triumph, but no doubt August was still there in spirit at least. No doubt about it at all. In a sense.

If Crime It Was

Had it not been for that washing, hanging out on that line to dry, in a small garden near the railway station, many years before your birth, though you might well never have visited the place anyway – which the mother who put it there finally got round to taking back in (it was already bone-dry and the air was not overwhelmingly clean) ten minutes after the crucial observer passed, then this planet, as a matter of fact, would have ceased to exist long ago. It turned out that that was the crucial point, and virtually no-one knew it. I did not even know it myself. Perhaps I found out eventually. That claim leads to rather a fraught issue, which I am reluctant to rehearse yet again just at present. But the unquestionable fact is that I didn't know that then, did I? Which is to say, at the moment I am just about to describe. There is unanimity on that point at least, which is always something.

What happened? Try to prevent me from telling you by all means if you wish. The decision is yours, after all – even though so few others are. For myself, this is how it happened. I heard a noise, and I ran out as quickly as I could, and I looked down the broad street. A consistent sequence of closely tailored actions, in other words. But there was no sign of anything suspicious in either direction I looked in. Nothing. Zilch. Niente. Ingenting. Starddenfagge. Then I thought: Well, why should there be – and returned to the interior of the shop. At which point, almost immediately after I had returned to the shop, but afterwards certainly, the great bell in the tower just down the street began booming. With every boom, most unusually, it continued to get, it seemed to me, louder and louder – a by no means usual state of affairs I remember thinking even as it was happening – until eventually, to everyone there's no small astonishment, it swung completely out and fell and landed in the street below. I refer to the bell, all of its workings, and most of its supports. I am trying to be as explicit as possible, you see. I am actually trying. I am actually trying. I insist that you give me the benefit of the doubt. You owe me at least that, you know. Honour your debts. What sort of a scummy world will it be otherwise, for God's sake? I am trying to communicate: can't you tell?

Where was I? Where were we? We did what anyone else would have done – certainly so if they had been us. Which is to say, we all ran out of our shops and we gathered at the still resonating site of the debris. Most of us were extremely shocked. One or two others, I confess, were already drunk. Nonetheless, we by and large marvelled at the fallen bell's uncanny size and extent. One of us, the one who sold prime slices of the past for a living – and a very comfortable living it was too, let me tell you, squire – although he did kill himself, purely for personal reasons, the following month – he said that it was truly a miracle that no-one had been killed in all the confusion and with all the flying debris and so forth. I thought of asking him just what he meant by 'and so forth' – quite a frequent reaction of mine nowadays, I observe. However, we noticed a severed head that was rolling slowly round and round the rim of the bell on the ground. Something must have finally released it. It is, after all, not the sort of detail that one can overlook forever. Some little old lady, out doing her little daily shopping, I suppose, caught by the blast. So we thought: oh well, what a pity. Apparently it isn't a miracle after all. Yet, it might well, I suppose, still be something pretty well like one, sort of, in a sense.

Someone remarked, rather sententiously, I thought – it must have been a passing spiritual adviser, I suppose, unless it was one who was specially sent as soon as possible to the scene of the crime: 'It is no doubt a tragedy that some people die. But how much greater a tragedy it would be for some people to live forever.' I felt this was rather ill-judged myself. It did not strike quite the right tone: the tone of sublime denial of the obvious. He clearly had certain specific people in mind. Or he knew that we would have. Then he said something about urination, if I heard him aright, which I confess I couldn't quite follow. What does it matter? All our religions are different ways into the same trackless wastes.

But, anyway, I didn't get much chance to think about it. The fact is that, just afterwards, almost before he had finished saying whatever it was he was saying, who should jump out of a passing car – a green one, as I recall – but Time himself? Smiling sheepishly, he came over to us and asked, 'How about that, eh? What do you say? Isn't Fate a bit of a bummer? Would you maybe like me to go into reverse?' Some of us hummed and hawed, and Mr Vico from the electrical goods shop – who is a crook, incidentally – looked to me very much as if he might raise his voice in favour of this nefarious and impossible under-taking. However, I was able to pre-empt him.

'We don't want any favours from you, Mr Time, you absolute shit,' I said forcefully, with an acerbity which even he, insensitive buffoon that he was, could not fail to notice. 'On your way. On yer bike. Out of it. Get. Va-moose. Scram.' And, faced with such unwavering and audacious enmity, he soon made himself scarce. I don't blame him. However, I cannot honestly deny that since then I have had some moments of doubt. Moments when I have thought: Maybe I really shouldn't have talked to him like that. After all, he is such a good ally to have on one's side, is he not, buffoon or no? Why make more trouble for yourself? But it was too late by then, of course. Anyway, the whole world split into four bits not three months afterwards, so it is quite possible it wouldn't have made all that much practical difference even so. Still, you never know, do you? It would be wrong to castigate oneself needlessly. Perhaps I am over-dramatising the whole thing. We are all guilty of that sometimes, I dare say. I certainly hope so. Oops. I have just fallen. That is happening more and more often nowadays. A worrying development indeed. Please help me get up, will you please?

A Cup of Rare Tea

A nondescript morning, but there was still much work to be done. The Romans sat in the tea house, gazing out dreamily towards the verandahs and pagodas beyond the lifting wooden eaves, and they wept or almost wept as they remembered the distant lands which had given them birth. Gradually their mood swings set in once again.

An obsequious local tradesman hurried out of the back door into the street beyond as they entered, bending his back excessively in an attempt at convincing subordination. A perfectly normal sight in these troubled times. But who knows what hatred he may have carried away in his heart?

Or perhaps he actually preferred things as they were. Who can say for sure? Possibly it was merely prudence on his part: the desire not to linger on the premises, lest this group of soldiers also grow maudlin and violent, and next start to demolish the interior of the gloomy if airy tea-shop with their bare hands, or their somewhat primitive weapons, out of sheer excess of energy as much as anything else.

After all, no-one doubted for a moment that this occupation would soon be over. That it could not be much prolonged. The army of loyal sons of the Empire at present massing to the north beyond the greatest of all rivers would soon enough reach an agreed plan, surely, and then sweep down from their strongholds across the great river to drive the large, cynical barbarians and all their engineering projects, however promising, off into the oceans and seas whence it is most likely they came. And it would soon once again be as if they had never even been there in the first place. The simple truth was that they had read the Five Classics and the Romans had not. No-one would miss them. Rightly were they called long-nosed barbarians.

'Old man! Senex! Hither!' cried G. Paulus Ventatus, espying a wizened face glancing out at him for obscure motives from behind the porcelain-filled rosewood screen beyond the counter. 'We have had enough of your un-convincing wines! Your table, however, convinces us. We are willing to pay in real bronze coins, stamped with the head of the last emperor but one, as far as we know anything about such things in this remote hell-hole out here.'

The old man did not move. He merely asked, inexpertly using the lingua franca of that broad area: 'What does the stinking shaggy gorilla of a round-eyed tyrannical bully-boy and his catamites want now?' But he used rather different words, of course. It was important not to lose sight entirely of the reality of the political situation.

'I'll tell you what me and my illustrious colleagues want. Get your youngest grand-daughter out here – we know she's back there; we've been watching you for quite some time. She is almost attractive. Get her out here dancing on this table and we shall pay you twenty-five arpagadi without demur. Take some of her clothes off, and we'll give you from thirty to fifty-five, depending on what we see. We have only sixty left at the moment. You see, Sinbod, me and the lads have been having a bit of an argument about one or two salient points and there is only one sure way to settle this. All right? Is it a deal? After all, we could just take anything we wanted gratis. We have the capacity, you know.'

'Sure thing,' said the old man, and he disappeared into the back of the shop, more keen than ever to witness the impending national salvation from this shameful condition of subjugation to a band of uncultured louts who had stumbled into a success which nothing in their present capacities had entitled or indeed enabled them to deal with. Would salvation never come? Forty years passed, and still he had not returned. The soldiers, mightily impatient by now, suspecting some sort of double-dealing, set up a roar until once again their plight had attracted attention from the interior of the establishment.

An old woman came out, her face a picture of disenchantment.

'Is our order', one of them cried, 'being seen to? I don't wish to be critical, but you do seem to be taking rather a long time over it. We are young men, you know.'

'Piss on out of it, Fart-face,' the old lady demurely replied, albeit in different words. She was, of course, the daughter in question, for whom the old man had gladly died long ago, rather than expose her to the threat of contempt and obloquy.

'What?' cried Valerius. 'Do you not realise who we are? Do you not understand that with one sweep of the arm of Rome, we could reduce you, your odoriferous dependants, and yea the great tea room here itself, to a heap of clinging, pestiferous rubble? We have many better brothels than this in Ostia, you know.'

'No,' replied the old lady. 'All of that escapes my

understanding. But I do understand that, while it lasted, Rome never quite got as far as here. Not by quite some way in fact. So how can you possibly expect me to be terrified by your threats? Prance on elsewhere, you sad and super-annuated nancy-boys.'

The men looked from one to the other, baffled. That is quite a good point, really, one of them whispered. A strong point, in fact. Let's leave. We needn't bother paying the bill, I shouldn't think, under the circumstances. They wouldn't recognise it. What do you say? There must be other places around here that we can go to.

I still say we should kill her and wreck the whole house, said Q. Lentulus Frato, whose brother was a praetor once. But the others went out to look for a convenient alternative anyway, and they did not come back either. And so the tea slowly grew cold, which was rather a pity.

A Classic Russian Novel

Trofim Ivanovitch Tsitstibogarvminmzhkhov had a magnificent and guilty secret. Unfortunately, for such is the unfathomable nature of the Russian soul, which foreigners cannot even begin to grasp, he had long ago entirely forgotten what it was. Therefore he left it to others to worry about it night and day and he contented himself with kissing medals, hugging the samovar, and prostrating himself before the icons. What choice had he? Indeed, let us try to learn from him as best we can ourselves, my brothers and sisters, you in particular, my companions in this sad world here below, where we wander friendless and lost between the silver birches. Ekh! This unending mud. Even his friend Shtine had to walk through this mud. But there is something good about it too.

Also, he worshipped God, though he quite often had very bad toothache – frequently for the whole day and much of the dark, howling night which followed, whether it was snowing or not, or whether it was he who was howling, or the night, or both of them – so he knew what pain was, and his life was at least not shallow and empty – such as, most usually, are those of the

Swedes and the Germans, and the inhabitants of Latin countries in particular; and of the inhabitants of many of our own great cities ('open sewers', I prefer to call them, fit for rats and certain other people, for, as the Good Lord so truly remarked, honesty is always the best policy). No, his life was full; was nearly always almost unbearably full. And of what use are lobsters anyway, my precious friends, when larger and subtler pincers are gnawing away at one's own inadequate heart?

Besides which, I too have suffered almost unbearably. The taste of lobsters is unknown to me, though perhaps, who can say, it was not always quite so; and, as for him, he killed a few old ladies, possibly, but no-one could sincerely deny that he was in essence profoundly spiritual and capable of wonderfully intense and prolonged bouts of introspection. What else can a Slav do? I mean to say: old ladies. After all, which of us is perfect? Well, me perhaps – but certainly not you. Time passes. I am ill. God bless the Tzar, and his sons and daughters too if they are good, which I should perhaps at once add I have not the slightest reason to believe they are not. Dear me, no. Even the torrential rainfall is blessed and silvery in this incomparable land of ours. Even our deaths are the only real deaths.

(Geneva–Lausanne–Paris–Rome.)

An Interrupted Autobiography

I have no reason to suppose that, as a child, I was any less observant than most. Indeed, to judge by the copious stock of memories which I already had by the age of ten or so, of various of my young female playmates inadvertently exposing themselves as they did one thing or another in our dingy, complex and sloping back green, frequently something that I had pretty carefully set up for them to do, I can only suppose that I probably tended to observe rather more than I ought to have done. Once or twice, I dare say, they did what they did advertently, but to me the feelings involved there were much different. It produced a sense of burning injustice which one knew it was not going to be easy to surmount. Indeed, it may even be that it proved to be impossible to do so.

Enough of this tedious scene-setting. Let us proceed in leaps and bounds. I hesitate to attribute my well-known passion for the pursuit of justice and the crushing of infamy to precisely those early experiences of mine. But who can truly tell? The dogs bark, and the men in the caravan shoot a few of them dead. Such is life. What else is it supposed to be like? And supposed to be by whom? The point was, whether or not I was more observant than most. All right. Listen to this. I think I can show quite clearly that I wasn't.

The fact is that the tenement in which I was brought up lay in busy streets at not more than five minutes distance from one of the largest and most astonishing buildings in the entire city. And a further, undeniable fact is that, when I left the city at the age of twenty-five, having (as I thought) explored a very good deal of it off and on during the years of my until then unpressed existence, I still did not know even that such a building existed! It is not, mark you, that I had never bothered to travel the ten or so minutes necessary for me to get a good, long look at it. It was not going to try to evade my gaze, after all. No, the point I am making, perhaps with less charm and allure than normal, I dare say, is that I actually did not even know that such a place existed. Its very existence had never been adequately brought to my juvenile attention. Have you grasped that? That is the point I was wishing to make. It would go against all the canons of good construction to repeat it a third time.

Good. Now, listen to this. I was spending my first night in the capital city of a neighbouring foreign country, when an American in the small bar of the hotel heard me saying something extremely witty and original to myself, and he correctly identified to me, in full public voice, my place of origin. I was taken aback not a little – but, even so, I would probably have been delighted by the exchange were it not for a sneaking suspicion that the American might be a sexual pervert of a particularly unwelcome type, or an obnoxiously religious person, or possibly both at once, as so many are nowadays. Certainly, there was something about his appearance which made me feel I could not risk being entirely unguarded in my conversation with him. He launched out, quite without preamble, into a long and impassioned disquisition in favour of my natal shores; and, when he found out more particularly where I was from, almost the first thing he mentioned was this spectacular building nearby, which he said had provided him with one of the fondest memories of his trip there. I refrained from enquiring which one. Apparently, in his capacity as a spiritual being, he accompanied various groups of decrepit religious tourists hither and yon, keeping an eye on their luggage, and trying (with great success) not to be seduced by them.

That was the last I saw of him, and his body was never subsequently found, although I dare say someone must have missed him. For myself, I was sufficiently intrigued to make a point of shortly afterwards seeking out the major reference library of the city I was in, and doing all I could to find out about this evidently wondrous edifice, the very existence of which I had somehow managed to overlook during an upbringing in the vicinity. I was fortunate to make the chance acquaintance of an admirably cheerful and assiduous worker in the bowels of the great chasm of lost volumes which lay at the heart of the library in question. His help was invaluable in directing me to the proper shelves. Alas, there was something in his attitude too that I did not warm to. I was, however, able to make my way out of the building unobserved, using the keys which I had taken from his pocket as he was lying prone on the floor, in a position where he would very likely not immediately be discovered. Such, alas, is life.

A few days later, quite by coincidence (or so I thought at the time) I received a letter from home. It mentioned, with some excitement – although it was not overmastered by it, since the relevant facts were put down only on the fourth page out of six – that that very same building (which it talked of as though I was expected to know it well) had been burned down overnight. Arson was suspected. Or an accidentally discarded cigar during a night of a form of public entertainment based on legalised violence. The sort of thing, in short, with which I have absolutely no truck and never have had throughout the extent of my entire existence.

Most peculiarly, the letter said, with a sort of resigned sigh, that no doubt none of us would ever be going there again. I do not remember that *any* of us *ever* went there. It ended by advising me against an immediate return home, confining itself to a few remarks about the dark suspicions which various unenlightened and uninformed people were evidently being much plagued by. We shall never betray you, it finished by insisting: a pronouncement which, I feel, rather defeated its own purpose. Much good may it do these intemperate and sanctimonious meddlers. This did not much impress me, as I had had no intention of going back there anyway at any time. I would certainly not be doing so now that our own special building had actually been destroyed in flames. People take so little care of other people's childhoods, or so I find.

Thus it was that I was tremulously approaching the age of forty-five, when – ach, fuckit, who cares in the slightest? I'll go and make myself a cup of coffee while I still can. Why is it over there by the fucking window? Fuck. Why must it too be so far away?

A Fragment Torn from the Age of the Great Cathedral Builders

And so, with a great and venerable guffaw, such as the limp, broken-backed men of today seldom laugh, since they have lost the knack of laughing today, in these doleful ages of doubt and swinish inactivity, he waited until the head of the godly clerk had appeared like a fearful moon sniffing at the window beside him before he lopped it off with a single fearful swing of his dauntless great sword, Leswingeur. And the body of the varlet, shocked, continued climbing up the ivy and disappeared at great speed onto and over the roof, the surprised head meanwhile toppling into the room and coming to a halt at the foot of the bed with a gasp, as it were, of mulish surprise. Whereat the Duke, waxing mighty in his rage, stamped over to the vast bed upon which his trembling, ashen daughter cowered, quaking and trying to hide behind a magnificently worked quilt which bore an image of the Eternal Virgin and her most celebrated child. But he, leaping up onto the bed with a great cry of successful vengeance, he with a single gesture thrust the integument aside and turned her nimbly over onto her trim stomach, and he did lift up with a shriek of noble triumph her goodly, starched night-dress, less pink and less white, and slightly more blue, than she was herself; and revealing thereby those incomparable globes to which the presumptuous clerk had dared to address some of the worst among his miserable lines of shitty verse – which is to say, her rump, bum, fudd, scutt, butt, fundament, seat, stern, hinder end, breech, backside, haunches, podex, nates, posteriors, hunkers, rear enchantments, reverse exquisencies, inverted spasmificent evolutions, or – not to mince words like a palsied, scent-drenched pagan – arse. And he took the discalced head of the miscreant, now severed from his puny, traitorous body, and he plunged its wet nose deep into the moist cleft of her swelling buttocks and he cried in his manifest glee, 'Is this then, whoreson dog, something of what thou thoughtest to do with the hitherto pure body of my only child, my incomparable Sengina, who is if anything even better-impedimented than her poor divine mother, the incomparable Lesbia; yea, she who died delivering her, when a heavy metal tankard full of the best wine in the country (valuable wine too, such as one would keep for a moment of the highest fitting celebration) dropped down onto her small and thrice unfortunate head from this very hand, so shaken was I by the joy of the occasion? Oh, what fit recompense this is for all my unimaginable sufferings until today!' For his lungs, be it noted, my fine fellow swivers and bed-pressers and mattress-collapsers were not, hear you, the puny, whimbling things such as the gelded popinjays of nowadays use for offering the sale of their most undesirable squitt-holes and other such bodily parts to each other in the numerous lanes and stews thrown up behind the crumbling, neglected aqueduct bequeathed to us from ignorant pagan antiquity, which we so rightly neglect or urinate against triumphantly on our way back from receiving the Blessed

Sacrament of Our Blessed Redeemer, whom the Jews hated because he was one of their number and was also so exceptionally good.

At which the decapitated head itself broke into a very hymn of praise of its own, a veritable cantus firmus, a spontaneous *'Te Deum'* of infinite gratitude, crying as it had done so, 'Yea, Master, what though I at present am spiritually and non-bodily in Heaven; yet does there nothing smell there as sweetly as this.' Whereat the Duke, in a rage, screaming 'Quartspasmold Whartingfast!' (which was the name of a lawyer whose privy members he was then using most ingeniously to hold up his much challenged breeches) did kick it mightily from his presence, out of the furthest opposite window, so that the unbodied head flew most expeditiously through the air and fell almost to earth, rudely hitting on the back of the skull a monk who was playing a fine old game in a field with a trio of rough farm labourers, a rope, and a few dead hedgehogs. And the monk died unshriven, in the height of his sins, which were considerable, it being a particularly bad moment for that sort of thing, from his point of view. But so things are. Man proposes, and God stuns him with a mallet. Such is how his infinite love expresses itself and who should know better than he how this is most properly to be done?

But all must work their way to salvation as best they can, my friends and fellow-drunks, if for some reason they are unable to purchase it. And thus it came about that the Duke, chancing to observe a maddening glimpse of the quaintly formed quoing of his normally quiet daughter thus marvellously displayed before him, as she squirmed in terror and loss, decided to forgive her. But to forgive one must first chasten, so that the merit shall be all the greater. Or perhaps the opposite. And

41

therefore it was, for the good of her immortal soul, that he subjected her to various sundry slight tortures which lasted long but left her after the shortest of pauses for recovery as good as in many parts unaffected. After which, sated and benign, he jumped into bed with her, performed a few saucy energetic acts which, without love between them, might have been called salacious by the unduly censorious; and then fell into mighty sound sleep, like the heroes of old, such as sleep all they who put their faith and trust in the efficacious sacrifice of that wondrous old trencherman and lover of all men and of one of his disciples in particular, the Jesus Christ, Our Lord, in whom we live and breathe and expel our wind and, to put it in another guise, pray. For naught happeneth without his implementation. And so may it go on forever. Which, indeed, it has no choice but to do. Amen, say we all, unless we are impotent believers in fairy tales from another district of the earth entirely, which (I dare answer for us both) we are not.

And verily, he died in the trust of the Lord; for, when his daughter was at last able to make her way out from under that manly magnificent part of him which had pinned her in place, and had removed her fierce bonds from some nine or ten delightful parts of her cruelly chafed apparatus, she ran off to a hidden shelf and took from it forthwith the most appalling poison, with which she had been meaning to kill herself if her plans to elope were thwarted by some unforeseen intervention, for such had been the extent of her unreasoning infatuation. And she poured this devilish elixir into his ears, nose, mouth, arsehole, and even attempted likewise to disfigure the tiny aperture which adorned his most needful part, through the wise disposition of the King of the Universe and designer of all things sensible and insensible, who takes a personal interest in everything. His judgement was swift. For, as she was so doing, the neighbours burned the castle down, since they had long been awaiting just such an opportunity, and they who were inside all perished in the flames, as indeed, for that matter, did all those who were outside, for a strange wind blew up just as they did so and swept through the entire country.

A Visit to the Office

When I at last got there, it was only to find that there was a note pinned to the door, saying that the office was closed for the rest of the day, in response to a private emergency. It very much regretted any inconvenience which this unexpected turn of events might occasion. It would be open again, it said, at the usual time tomorrow morning.

This was, to say the least, an unexpected development. I had carefully carried out all the preliminary work, all the checking and counter-checking, all the signing, and stamping, and quarrying-out of long-mummified information and so forth, so that the forms would be in impeccable order, and the assignment would require nothing more than for me to turn up before the agreed close of day with everything just as it should be. I would then simply hand over all the stuff and it would be out of my hands. I would be shot of it. I would have done my bit. Events could proceed on their natural course well out of my sight. I could then just slope off and enjoy myself until something else turned up that required to be done, awaiting with no small confidence a successful outcome to my modest labours.

All right, I was leaving it a bit late. You might say that that is the risk you take. But what risk? There were advertised opening hours. It's a public office, for God's sake. You expect it to be open to the public at the stated hours. You expect to be able to rely on that. What sort of society would it be if all the post offices and banks and so forth could simply shut down at will following the whims of the various lickspittles, froth-blowers and fatarses that worked there? It is simply not a workable arrangement. There are rules, after all – are there not?

Well; no. Evidently not. It seemed that, thanks to some far-off personal disaster of which I knew nothing, I was going to miss the deadline after all. That this would cause problems for me very probably far far exceeding whatever it was that had temporarily closed down the office in the first place obviously did not make a fleabite of difference. I would just have to put up with it. It could kill me, for all anyone else cared.

Of course, I did not even know for sure that this supposed emergency that had cropped up really was an emergency at all. More likely than not, it had been getting towards the end of a slack afternoon, they had looked at each other from the depths of their various tediums, or perhaps tedia, and a mutual decision had been silently born. Let's all just eff on off out of here, and if anybody else has the poor taste to turn up in our absence, well then, sod him, her, it, or them. Goodbye, cruel world. Right. So off they went. I have a certain sympathy with them, I don't deny that. And, of course, I happened to be the first one who did turn up afterwards. Of course I was. How could it have turned out differently? The entire universe had obviously been tending towards this point since at least the last Ice Age. It is probably the very reason why the gases converged towards solidity all that absurd amount of time ago.

If ever they did. Fortunately, when I went away to find someone to complain to – which I did, volubly – I found out that it had been entirely the wrong office anyway that I'd been trying to get into. I was thus able to hurry up to the right place and hand in the completed forms with a few minutes to spare after all. I could then proceed with my life thereafter as I had originally intended to. That was a relief. There is a very obvious moral to all this, needless to say, and that is, not to hang about wasting time in repining and moaning about your fate, but instead to go ahead and try to do something positive about it. Had I waited for much longer outside the wrong door, the proper office would have shut for the day too. And where would I have been then? It hardly bears thinking about.

As I passed the first office again on the way out, I saw someone else standing in front of it, gazing at it with a fairly aghast expression on his face. I very nearly told him of my own experience, but I decided against it. It is always better, I feel, to let people find out things for themselves. It's the only way one ever learns anything, really. Sometimes help is not really what people are requiring. Not in the deepest sense. In fact, if you asked them, they would probably tell you that they wanted to be left alone anyway.

I intend to ignore the rather arrogant request which was made to me, asking me to make some financial contribution towards offsetting the cost of necessary repairs to the damage. I gladly concede that they did have the different identifying numbers and so forth on all the various doors; and so I suppose, technically, I was perhaps at fault for going to the one with the wrong number on it – but the fact was that the emergency notice to some extent obscured the important information which was given on the woodwork beneath it. At the very least, this shows extremely bad planning on their part. At times I think it is almost a conspiracy to mislead, and perhaps even to exploit, the public. Still, one doesn't want to get paranoid.

Clarke Kunte

The unveiling of the controversial statue of *King William of Orange and the Pope engaged in an Act of Indecency with the Angel Gabriel* on its fine high plinth on the Clyde Walkway near the railway bridge in Glasgow was, most unexpectedly, made the occasion for scenes of public affray among the normally calm, philosophical inhabitants of that stately burgh universally lauded nowadays from Bearsden to Giffnock as the Imperial Rome of the North. The artist, the controversial English symbolist Sir F. Whipsnade Prance, was humanely enough beheaded, all things considered, and his corpse was tossed into the river in a manner carefully calculated not to inconvenience the breeding habits of the local wildlife. It had always been held by some of the town's major critics, right from the start, that the artist could have no idea quite what he was getting himself involved in, and that he would very likely not prove to be sufficiently sensitive to what they liked to refer to as a complex dialectic of local needs. Such people held that the commission therefore ought by rights to have gone to one of the many superbly gifted indigenous artists with which the city was (and still is) thronged almost to surfeit. Some of them even live there. These critics, not unnaturally, felt themselves to be entirely justified by the ensuing course of events.

As for the artist's head, it was used for an impromptu kickabout on the quayside, which the army was eventually called in to disrupt with the score at 3–3, to the considerable resentment of both sides, each of which felt itself to be the team more likely to produce the winning goal. Such is life. Six goals in eighty-five minutes, however, quite apart from the ten or so strikes which had been disallowed for one reason or another – usually, but not invariably, the illegal use of firearms – does at least suggest a most exciting match.

But by this time the main brunt of the battle was raging in another part of the city. Pitched fighting had spread across the bridge and, by a singularly unfortunate disposition of a benign but inscrutable Providence, it had reached and spilled over into the forecourt of the large mosque which was situated just south of the river. Of course, none of this had anything to do with religion as such; with religion in the true sense of the word. How could it have had? Religion is always the good stuff. Nonetheless, for convenience and succinctness of reference, it may perhaps not be too inaccurate to say that whereas before it had solely been a fraternal battle between Catholic Christians and Protestant Christians, in which both sides, doubtless misguidedly, had been causing deaths and serious injuries in honour and praise of the same God, at this point the local Muslims joined in and the whole affair, frankly, took a rather ugly, comparative-religion turn.

Particularly bearing in mind the presence of a synagogue nearby, which young men bearing clubs and flaming torches were beginning both to approach and to emerge from – little though this too had to do with religion in the true sense of the word either – it is hard to say what the ultimate issue might not have proved to be, had it not been for a most unexpected intervention which now took place. Nearly everyone must know what this was, but I shall repeat it nonetheless for the sake of completeness. One of the large tower-blocks nearby, needless to say, with its many thousands of inhabitants, suddenly swayed and fell over loudly and neatly onto its side. Crashing to the ground, it perfectly annihilated precisely the area in which all the still warring factions were congregated, hammering the contenders into the ground as it did so, missing none of them, and thereby instantly exchanging all the turmoil for peace of a sort, including in many cases immediate burial. So: is there a providence looking after us or is there not? You tell me.

Of course, all the people in the houses died too in the same operation, but if Providence, which can do everything possible, could possibly have arranged things in a fairer way, no doubt it would have done; although it might actually have chosen to employ what was the fairest possible way anyway, and very probably did, for who are we to judge and interpret the actions of Divine Providence? Of course, we do it all the time, as a matter of fact; but we can be confident that it is utterly beyond us even so. After all, what else can we do? It is always so easy to sneer, and point to real difficulties in religion as if somehow they were real difficulties. That is merely to take the simple way out, which is so typical of the scientific attitude.

We may, however, I think discount as absurd and impossible some of the most incredible of those reports which began circulating within minutes of the event in question. Mere contemporaneity, as any devout student of history knows, is not everything. Far from it. Some of the most marvellous accounts of the most wondrous events in our spiritual history did not, through the grace of the Almighty, emerge into the light of day until many long centuries after the events which they so assiduously and accurately describe. Here I refer particularly to those who claimed that it was not a single building which fell, but in fact two or three of them. And also to those who claimed that whatever number of buildings might have fallen, they had in fact, one or many, been pushed over.

In short, there were those so troubled in mind as to have claimed to see a peculiarly-garbed figure, of only slightly more than life size, if even that, and evidently able in some manner to fly. He it was, they claim, who was pushing against the top of the building and causing it by his main personal strength to topple over onto the dis-putants beneath. We need, I feel, have little compunction in dismissing this story out of hand as being self-evidently legendary or fraudulent. These things, pretty obviously, just do not happen. How can they? As for those misguided souls below who claimed to see this figure appearing at the time, a being for whose existence we have only the extremely limited testimony of what amounts to no more than five hours of filmic footage, videos, a couple of hundred photographs and perhaps two or three dozen eye-witness accounts, these are to be regarded more in pity than anger as being genuinely deluded in mind, extremely credulous to boot, and quite possibly consti-tuting a genuine danger to the health of the common-wealth.

We must by all means try to be fair. Nonetheless, we may, I think, be quite certain, no matter what a few profoundly misguided zealots might wish to claim, for reasons best known to themselves (or not), that there simply is no such person as this supposed Clarke Kunte of theirs, whom they pretend has supernatural powers, and who will hasten to the defence of the followers of what they, in their insanity, are pleased to call the oldest and yet the most modern and mature religion of all, and one uniquely well suited to the requirements of the present age: to wit, Kunteism. One need merely state all this in the barest of outline for its futility and absurdity to be brought home to one. If he exists, for instance, why doesn't he strike me dead at the present moment? Right now. Why doesn't he do it right now? See. He didn't. He couldn't. There is simply no such being. And another thing.

Bald Sandy

I t was when all the villagers had gathered down at the
lakeside, helping to perform the ancient monthly spiritual ceremony of loading the archbishop's barge with as
much food and drink as it would hold, that the astonishing phenomenon which was occurring simultaneously at
the top of the hill was first noticed. 'Look!' cried one of the
poor farmers, pointing up to the church at the very peak,
the building they had so recently filed out of en masse,
praying and screaming. 'Look at our sainted church! It is
rising into the sky and it is already vibrating there! How
could the heretics or atheists conceivably hope to explain
this? Victory is ours at last!'

A gasp ran through the assembled multitude. They
looked, and they saw. All of them saw the undeniable
miracle, even the girl who was blinded by it and the
ancient married couple who, overcome by joy, succumbed to their heart conditions and toppled unnoticed
over the promenade wall. Splish! Splash! The church at
the top of the hill had at some point after their recent
departure undeniably risen up into the air. No-one
doubted it. There was a thin but quite noticeable gap
between its base and the level of the ground where it had

previously and apparently contentedly rested. It was all so obvious that there could be no possibility of an error.

The crowd broke out into loud sobs and cries of praise. There were calls of, 'Photograph it! Photograph it before it goes away!' – 'Film it!' – 'No! No! Get it on video! That would be much better! Over there! Get out of the way, you bloody fool! Get your hands off them!' – and people hurried around trying to get this done in good time. Alas, most unfortunately, through a sort of baleful fatality which continually haunts such endeavours, none of these innumerable attempts came out clearly enough to pro-vide conclusive proof to the pig-ignorant who were minded to deny the truth of the unanimous reports. It would perhaps have been better to have made no such attempts at all. Why play the doubters at their own game? Those who refuse to believe will refuse to believe, no matter how good the evidence is. It's in their nature. They can't help it. As one of the greatest of all converts pointed out, a turd is a turd is a turd. It is therefore rather beside the point to seek to provide them with good or convincing evidence. To know that the truth is truly the truth is surely enough.

At once a stampede ensued, as the faithful sought to get back up the hill to their supernaturally bombinating ecclesiastical edifice before it could gently settle back, as always seemed the likeliest end-result, into a routine and quiescent state. One or two even fell by the wayside, and were succoured by followers who were too ancient or asthmatic to climb as quickly as the others. The beautifully sculpted arcades fluttered like the stone frills of a skirt of a leaping and dancing maiden. Alas, her titties were well hidden, but, according to more than one report, the doorway glinted darkly as it shook about very like her exquisitely bemused anus. The window gleamed like her

56

innumerable eyes. The inspired spire waggled like – well, to be quite frank, like some sort of misplaced angelic penis, whether angels are females or not. It was that sort of vision. There is little to be achieved by shying away from the actual facts. There rarely is. Let us proceed with condign dignity. Pick up that disgusting object at once.

Alas, when the first of the faithful arrived back and tried to throw themselves humbly and self-abasingly underneath the church as a sign of the depth and buoyantly uncritical nature of their proud and mature beliefs, they found that the building had already settled very solidly back onto the ground again. Thus for their devoted pains they received little more than abrasions or splitting headaches or injured skulls as they hurled themselves fearlessly against the firm low skirt of the church-wall. But they were nothing daunted by this unfortunate miraculous transience. It was, in a sense, only what was to be expected under the circumstances. What is bliss without pain, after all? Gathering their renewed spirits warmly together under the guidance of their ecclesiastical mentors, they flowed on into the church itself, quacking and whooping, quaking and shivering, eager to embark on a spontaneous ceremonial service of thanksgiving. 'Oh Lord,' intoned the dignitary in the high pulpit at the climax of these grateful proceedings. 'We know. We know what we saw. We know what we saw, for we saw it. No-one else saw it, or could see it. But we did. We did not just imagine it. Therefore we believe. Not because we are stupid or hysterical or obtuse or dull of vision. Not at all. For why should such prodigies also be vouchsafed to unbelievers? That would surely rob them of much of their mystique and their mystical point. But we know what we saw nonetheless. Hysteria is for others. And the carping of miserable and hopeless sinners, perverts, cheats, sneerers, committers of incest and social parasites will not budge us one iota from our certainty that we saw what we did undoubtedly see. So – up theirs for a kick-off. And we shall carry on our lives secure in the truth of this assumption. For we are much relieved and greatly to be relied on. For we know the truth of all this event, and therefore we are blithe and gay. Amen. Pass the plate round.'

And the crowd answered, in one voice, a loud and magnificent 'Amen!' And some said, 'What?' However, not all the village was quite there. For there was a lame man among them who took much longer to reach the church than did all the others. And his name was Alexander, for Alexander was the name of him, and so was he called, for such was his name, whereas other names, quite simply, were not. Except for his second name, which was Constantine. And his first name was Alexander, as I have perhaps already mentioned. It was also the name of his name. As also were Sandy, Sawn, Alex, Alec, Aleck, Al and Baldy. For he was very bald. Truly, he was bald. As an egg. As the numerous private parts in a harem. And he arrived, gasping and limping, in the small square in front of the church much later than did any of the others, and it was entirely deserted but for him, for the rest were inside the sacred building, screaming and hollering out their mature testimony to their faith. Whereas he was not. He was outside. For that is where he was. Nor was his skull covered in hair.

And as he crossed the square as quickly as he could towards the church, he heard above himself a voice say 'Sandy!', and he looked up, and he saw a person who filled much of the sky above himself. But it was done in a beautiful and affectionate manner. And she was lovelier to him even than the evening clouds, when the sky is full of warm veins of gold and the life of the day for a while seems wondrous beyond all improving. Begob. And that celestial person was a female who was younger than she looked. And he said, 'Oh Jings!' and he fell to the ground, and when he was lying on the ground, lo, he said 'Oh Jings!' again, in a voice quieter than before. For he was much amazed. Beyond belief, in fact.

And the woman said to him, 'Sandy! My dearest Baldywaldy. Why sayest thou "Jings!"? For there is no need. I am here to bless and help you. Or thee, if I may. I am here to dignify your life to an extent beyond your dreams and even your greatest dreams, and I shall do so. You just watch. For look, I am the friend of you and of all of you and of all who believe like you. Have a look at this if you don't believe me. Go on. What about that? Tell me what you honestly think. Eh?'

Whereat she lifted up the deepest and innermost hems of her ancient and not over-clean mantle, and Alexander staggered back like one both delighted and afraid. For he was extremely delighted, and even more extremely afraid. But most of all he was amazed and enchanted. For, to his immense gratification and surprise, she continued to lift the hem until her legs and then more than her legs were visible, well above the neat knees, yea, even to the navel, which is by the vulgar (who surely scarcely deserve to see it) called the belly-button. And he saw that her belly-button was pretty, and he was mightily pleased thereat. It was what he had until then by and large taken for granted. But who can, in the darkest embraces of the night, entirely annihilate lowering and doubtful thoughts? Not me, Bud. Nor Sandy neither. It humanises us, I tend to think.

Wherewith she fell back in the cloud-filled sky and spread her legs akimbo, to demonstrate to him her private parts, now less private than they had been hitherto. And Sandy looked, and lo, he beheld her divine appurtenance or, not to mince words, twat. And he said, Oh, it reminds me of someone but I cannot just at the moment remember whose. (But he knew perfectly well whose.) For I am an old man and my memory fails me at just the wrong moment and my private parts are of less general advantage to me and my kin than once they were. But it is all so unbelievably pretty anyway. Don't think I'm not incredibly grateful, because I am. I really and truly very much am. Oh yes. Very much so, Missis.

And a great fear came over him nonetheless, for he knew he would very likely have to pay dearly for something like this. Nor, as the event showed, was he very much wrong in this sad conclusion. For such is how it usually proceeds. And she said: How about this, eh? Incomparable or what? Beautiful or just sensationally beautiful? I mean, be honest. And he, sensing that etiquette expected a reply from him, agreed in broadly the same words. And she asked: Tell me this, Mister. Where else would you expect a god to come out of? And he replied humbly, as was befitting, that it was certainly, as far as he could tell, the most externally appropriate place for such an event to occur in by a long way. And he hoped against hope that she would not further enquire as to just what he meant by that rather peculiar remark. And he was rewarded. For she, evidently much moved, merely sighed a little, and let's a brief spasm of warm, friendly liquid fall onto his head. And in a moment more she had utterly departed.

Whereat Alexander, not even staying to wipe himself clean or dry, for that would (so he thought) have smacked of a particularly repellant blasphemy, hurried as best he could into the cathedral, where the thanksgiving celebration was even then drawing to its natural close. And he interrupted them and he called out, Behold! It is I! And they cried, It always is! It is Alexander! Yea, even he who is oft jocularly amongst us known by the appellation of Baldy! So what? And he cried out and said, I bring you news! Great news! A visitation! A vision of wonder and delight, the like of which has never I think been seen in the sky over any other part of the earth! A rare cracker and no mistake! And he fell to the ground, exhausted, in his overpowering sense of achievement and joy. And he began to snore, such as he often did at nights, to the great discomfiture of his still highly admirable wife Virginia. Or Constance, if Virginia is dead. Which I very much hope not.

And they revived him, and they carried him to the altar-rail, and he stood there. And he raised his voice in incomparable exaltation, for he knew that he was in the profoundest sense the favoured one and the chosen one. And in as few words as he could he sought to tell them of all that he had so recently witnessed. And his eyes shone with an unearthly light, testifying to the glory and the certainty within his faithful heart. Nor did he even notice the beginning of the first murmurs against him, after some minutes had passed, so elated and inspired was he in his joy.

And as they began to realise what he was claiming to have seen, there broke out moans and cries and eldritch shrieks in the congregation, along the lines of, 'Jesus H. Strich!' and 'Satan himself has taken possession of his revolting talking apertures!' and 'The Holy Father's penis, cut into slices, and served in a frying-pan!' (which is a common expression in Quebec, or so I am told, when one is taken aback) and 'Can this somehow also be possible?' And they began to throw things at him, and they jumped upon him, and they thus soon silenced him.

And the High Priest (whose name was, as usual, Kenneth) ascended swiftly to the highest point of the church and he cried out to them, 'Lo! Let us be vigilant! Only the authority of an established church can help you in such a dilemma. Or what? Specifically, this one. For who among you would seek to deny that it is perfectly conceivable, yea, and possible to see a cathedral swaying about in the upper air? That is something which all men would concede to be possible. Whereas to see a holy woman demonstrating her delightfully aromatic snatch to you up in the sky somewhere is an abomination and an outrage and a sin; and those who imagine such things are sick to the core and they must be punished for it, lest they prove a scandal and a stumbling-block to the faithful. Also, people need their simple and innocent pleasures. It is I myself who has said this.'

And Alexander thought, pinned below a pile of angry bodies, I very much repent my openness. It was ill-judged. For I do not much like the way in which this seems to be developing, neither do I wish I were here. And yet I am here indeed. For my room at home is warm and quiet, and my dog Bongo will soon expect me back with food. He may well be whimpering already. And I have obviously miscalculated badly, for the truth that I have seen does not seem to be adequate for these strange and incensed people. And he was unquestionably right, as far as he went.

And the High Priest said, What shall we do with this cleg, this masturbator, this liar, this exhibitionist, this pervert and this fornicating whore or whoreson? Choose in the righteousness of the Lord, and whatever you choose I shall obey your commands, providing they are licit. Let it not be for me to judge him, but let it be for you to do so. And they huddled together for a while and then called out, 'Cut off his foreskin!' And the priest did so, with an unsettling grin. And they said, some of them, 'In fact cut off his entire —g!' And he did. 'And his scrotum too!', they shouted. And he did that too. After which their inspiration seemed to flag a little.

However, it was the case that Alexander was by then in a condition which none envied and very few regretted so that even his widespread baldness now seemed by comparison to be a trivial thing. And they came to themselves and cried out, Drag him to the highest point of the city and throw him therefrom for his arrogance and his dishonesty and the bad moral example which he has displayed unto our young ones; for he has become like unto one of those who blaspheme and say that we judge what the gods can do and cannot do, whatever infinity we claim to give them, or the gods are our invention and our own invention only. So let us gaily prong his whodger. After which, to be realistic, there was not much hope for him.

And so they did that too. And that was, in short, what happened to Alexander. So try to remember that when next you have a vision, lest you inadvertently say the wrong thing to the wrong people. For who decides what is truly from God and what is not? Although, of course, if nothing is actually from God and that is the simple truth of the matter, then what – but I threaten to digress. Anyway, I am too tired to continue. I am very tired. I suppose, to you, I am dead; but to me at the moment I am just extremely tired. Raining again.

Crossing the Threshold

I was just coming out of a second-hand bookshop in Great Western Road, when I happened to bump into a cousin of mine whom I hadn't seen for a long time. In fact, at first I didn't even recognise her. I would quite happily have stridden right past her after my brief and almost abstract apology, with no sense of anything else being required of me, but her powers of instant identification were fortunately better than mine and she stopped me by tapping my shoulder and correctly naming me.

For a moment I thought, Good heavens! At last I am beginning to have the effect on random, not unattractive females which I surely deserve to have. Then she identified herself as my cousin, Moira, and she told me again who I was from her point of view, which was impressive and fairly decisive; so I stopped to have a brief blether with her, even though as far as I knew she was off living in Australia somewhere. One does one's bit, after all.

She asked me if I had bought anything when inside the shop. I answered with a fairly noncommittal affirmative, since I don't much like such phoney smalltalk. Gamely ploughing on, she asked me what it was I had just bought. I took the easiest way out and merely showed her my purchases, giving as little as possible of a commentary on them. An exciting modern novel, dirt-cheap and possibly worthless. Also, a book of old pictures of the city – including, as it happens, as I discovered only later, a view of almost exactly what we could have seen had we glanced to the right from that very doorway, to a vista practically unchanged after ninety years, except for the clothing styles and the specific positioning of most of the people and vehicles. And lastly, there was yet another book which promised, no doubt mendaciously, to throw open the innumerable closed doors in the palace of mathematics to the serious searcher after their truths.

That settled, I thoughtlessly asked her what she herself was doing going into a bookshop. This remark needed to be instantly apologised for, of course; although, given the little I knew of her, it was a not unreasonable enquiry to make. She brushed it lightly aside, evidently unoffended. Anyway her mind was on other things rather. She said she had been chosen to give birth to God himself, and that she was therefore going in to see if they had a book of names. Nothing but the best. After all, she wanted to choose the right name for him when he arrived – or one that was at least not inappropriate. An emissary from beyond the spheres of time and space, she added, or from one of the places beyond there, had visited her that very morning – it was a beautiful, bright day, as I remember – in the spacious room she was now renting near the Botanic Gardens, to reveal to her the impending earth-shattering and epoch-making event. It had evidently left the choice of a name up to her – no doubt to give her some scope for making a direct contribution of her own to the business, presumably lest she might otherwise have felt rather put upon. Get people to assume the responsibility for something, and much of your work is done. These beings understand human psychology, I think we have to take that as read.

I found some of this rather puzzling; but I had gathered that she was pregnant and so I congratulated her on it, since this is the sort of thing one does in civilised society. To be honest, I had absolutely no idea of what the state of play was in her private life. However, she seemed glad to be congratulated, which was nice. For a moment, we regarded each other in silence. There didn't really seem to be all that much else to say.

'Takes some believing, doesn't it?' she asked, as much to say something, I felt, as for any weightier reason. 'Nonetheless, there it is. Unless I am seriously misinformed, which I doubt – for for why would anyone want to do that? – many billions will believe in whatever-I-call-him both here and elsewhere on other continents all down the centuries. Someone has to do it, after all, no? I mean, what other sort of people actually exist except real ones? Oh well. Might catch you later.' Then, with a cheery goodbye, she turned briskly and made her way into the shop in pursuit of what she clearly thought was a major part of her quest. And I dare say she was right.

I thought of following her in, but I was already a bit late. The fact is I had been home late yesterday too, and I very definitely did not want a repeat of the (I suppose) reasonable degree of aggression which not turning up in time ('Merely to eat the food – when it's rarely if ever you who has to make it') might provoke. Was that it? The thing is, for the last four or five years I had taken it for granted that she had been settled down in Sydney or Melbourne or Brisbane or one of those places. All very odd. Also, she always did have, as far as I remember, a rather odd sense of humour. Still. Perhaps I can get somewhere this time in my attempts to get closer to the world of mathematics. One lives in hope, does one not? Well, yes; I suppose one does. The endless pursuit of truth. That sort of thing. All the time, if one can manage it; but, if not, then certainly in one's leisure hours. That is the least one can do.

Smifth

We have all done strange stuff in our time, no doubt, but the thing is I had only sort of gone in there to get out of the rain. I used to go to the auction rooms quite often at one time in my life. For instance, I remember I used to have an artist friend who lived just round the corner, a very gifted man he was too, though soon afterwards he became magnificently successful and went off over the Atlantic and deteriorated more quickly than you could ever have thought possible.

Not that I should really have been surprised by that. The sad fact is, as he himself used to say often enough, that it was normal for artists – it seemed to set in almost to an epidemic extent towards the end of the nineteenth century – once they had gone some way through their apprentice phase and had at last blossomed into what they thought was their maturity, it was normal for them to start painting work which was far more aware and theoretically-grounded than their earlier stuff, and also, alas, far less interesting to look at. Mind you, this is not exactly what happened to Smifth. Like many modern artists, he did not seem to have had an apprentice phase. Or he had nothing else, with no guarantee of a qualified trade at the end of it.

69

Dear old Smifth. You know, I doubt if I had thought of him more than once or twice in the last fifteen years. What the memory does to us! Which is to say, even by leaving us alone. At one time we used to meet regularly, several days a week. He told me once that, in his opinion – I think he had very recently been drinking, which was no rarity – he believed that the destruction of the Euston Arch marked the climax of the cosmos, the *Abfallspunkt*, the moment at which the peak of the existence of the universe had been reached, and that thereafter it must of necessity be downhill all the way. At first (this was perfectly normal too) I was not at all sure what it was he was talking about; but apparently there had once been a huge elaborate archway structure outside Euston Station in London, and he had had happy memories of being at it about to travel, in pretty extreme youth, about to embark on a memorable journey. Or possibly on various journeys. He must have meant, if he meant anything at all, that the destruction of the Arch was the first step of the infinite falling away. Quite from what I am not sure.

Dear old Smifth. Discretion and sensitivity to the preferences of others were not, you might say, his ruling passions. He had this terrible habit of talking in a voice which was only slightly louder than normal, but strangely penetrating, particularly when (as, it must be said, very often happened) he had drunk rather more than was ideally good for him. I used to write some of his remarks down later, if I remembered to do so, and could remember what they were. Often, of course, I didn't. I am still wholly unsure, for instance, what it was that occasioned: 'One thing I will say about Raphael. Not only did he have a pretty solid technique, but he certainly painted some of the funniest pictures anyone could ever hope to see.' I turned that up in an old notebook years later. Maybe

Raphael was mentioned in a catalogue. Obviously no Raphaels ever turned up at the sort of sales we used to go to. Not unless it was someone else called Raphael, which is just possible, I suppose. At one point I was nearly called Raphael myself. However, these auction meetings were all far more downmarket than that. It may have had something to do with bodies travelling through the air.

Not that he was infallible either. I well remember how once he was going on and on about the obvious and palpable authenticity of a particular work, which he seemed to me to be showing a ridiculous degree of partiality for, a wide view in the Low Countries, of which one has seen thousands in one's time – until I directed his attention to a blunt remark in the accompanying litera-ture which made it clear that the artist had certainly never been to the place in question in his entire life. He hadn't even been to the *country* in question in his life. Or, presumably, out of it. He was working from a pre-existing known etching, which had been made by someone else. Smifth thanked me for this information in a voice slightly less flamboyant than usual, rather like an advocate ex-pressing gratitude to a judge for having just ruined his case by his crude and wholly superfluous intervention. It is hardly a coincidence, he said bitterly, that no-one since the dawn of time has ever said anything witty about landscape etching. 'Or perhaps you know a few jokes on that subject, do you?' he asked me, with a considerable degree of irritation on his voice. 'Not as such,' I replied carefully, choosing to avoid a direct confrontation.

More typical of him, perhaps, was the time when he greeted yet another religious picture with the generously volumed remark that it should have been immediately obvious to everyone concerned that there was something very wrong with this Judas fellow when they saw that he

71

was the only one in the company who wasn't wearing a halo. I also remember how he once dismissed a very tasteful Victorian essay in the realms of sub-pornography which pretended to be about Purity and Virtue and so forth with the lethal observation that the main problem with painted nudes in this genre is that none of them actually smell. I asked him, What painted nude ever does, except perhaps of paint? He smiled abstractly and pretended not to have noticed that I had said anything. That was not, I must confess, the only time I ever caught him doing that. Indeed, I remember only now how once he said to me: 'I shall have to leave the country soon, Porter. The fact is you are simply too quick for me.' At the time I had simply thought this was a joke.

Anyway, as I say, I had used to go to the auction rooms quite often, but I had gotten out the way of it for the last few years. There was also the fact to be considered that I had really no other very likely cause to be finding myself down in that part of the city-centre at mid-day on a Friday. But on this day I happened to be thereabouts checking out some applications for my computer, and the skies just about opened, and it was quite like old times when I saw a few people slipping into the Auctioneers' Rooms. So I thought I might as well go in there myself. Fortunately, they seemed to have forgotten who I was. There were a whole lot of little portraits there, old, and of people who were completely unknown. Not a single name seemed to have survived anywhere about any of them. Could this be true? Unknown people, usually drawn by barely known or equally unknown artists. Eerie. But I couldn't afford to think about that for too long. The fact is I had had this meal earlier in the day which internally I was growing more and more unhappy about. With very good reason, as it soon turned out.

Several Million Realistic Novels

If I were to try to explain to you just how it is that I managed to move in a single day from the slums of one of the poorest quarters of town, with their extremely disobliging inhabitants and their many boarded-up windows, to a fine park-viewing apartment in this exquisite district, next door to some nice quiet people, all thanks to the combined operation of a hammer, a dead vole, a very long pair of ladders, and a little box the contents of which rattle as one shakes it, I doubt very much indeed whether you would believe me. I do indeed have my doubts. Which is perhaps just as well, since it would not be entirely true. Most would no doubt be true, yes; yes; most would be true. I don't deny that. But not quite all. That is the thing. That is what I am saying.

So I'll tell you what I did instead. Instead, I wrote it all down laboriously in a manuscript during my leisure hours, and I placed this when I had finished it in a large box which I have put under the bed I have slept in for these last four decades, near enough – very far under the bed, right back against the wall. Right back there. This my heirs will no doubt discover when I am dead. It will be up to them to decide what to do with it. I like to think they will read it lovingly and laboriously, one word after the next, which is much the best way to read; but my fear is they will simply toss it out with the garbage as just one more item of the near infinite rubbish which so clutters up my life in particular and this utterly wonderful world of ours in general, which is in some ways worse than it was in my young day, and, I can hardly deny it, in some ways better too. Oh. And now, if you'll excuse me, I must go to answer a knock on the door. If I don't come back soon, please continue without me. Allow me to whistle while I disappear from view, I beg you. I have always found that that helps a great deal. Thank you.

The Best I Can Do

At that time, as I can still very well remember, we used to meet on several various mornings of every month in that magnificent disused church by Archibald 'Egyptian' Thomson that is still standing at the top of the hill in Saint Vincent Street. (At least, it was still there when last I looked.) There were all sorts of things that used to go on there in those mornings – those bright, hopeful mornings – although it was all very responsibly and discreetly done, of course. It had to be. If the authorities at that time had got wind of even half of it, we would all have found ourselves in serious trouble. In very serious trouble indeed. In fact, as far as I can remember, some of us did so anyway.

I used to be one of the people – we were nearly all of us men – who dressed up in the old garb and processed around the interior of the secretive kirk chanting the old chants, dancing the old dances, and singing the old songs. Sometimes we would also curse the old curses. After the rituals – and to some extent, in some cases, during them too – we would likewise think the old thoughts as best we could and drink the old drinks.

It was a fairly loose organisation. The criteria for membership were in themselves strict – you had to be able to convince the elders that you were genuinely willing to work for the restoration of all that had once been ours in the local environment – but the ritual always seemed to me to have something haphazard and thrown-together about it, and often it trembled on the verge of collapsing into an embarrassing heap of contradictory movements and general chaos. Indeed, embarrassment was very often an undeniable accompaniment to all our endeavours there, which were, if I may be allowed to say so at this juncture, now that first rapture has long since cooled, usually markedly higher on enthusiasm than on practical value. Quite simply, although we wished our actions to be as authentic as possible, to a considerable extent we had not the least idea what we really ought to have been doing for this to be the case.

Nonetheless, although there are some who say that nothing of any value in the slightest was ever achieved there, my own estimate of the results of that unquestionably sincerely meant movement is far more positive. And I believe (I certainly hope) that I would think this even without the immense benefits which taking part in the meetings brought to my personal life. I know also from my own experience that the organisation happily allows those who feel that their own ways of thinking have moved on, to distance themselves without rancour from their former friends, activities, and acquaintances, after only a minimum period set aside for readjustments, attempts to persuade, payment of forfeits, tearful prayers, very mild physical chastisement, and so forth. It is all so wonderfully civilised nowadays, now that the more heroic ages have passed.

For me, of course, the one central fact about it all is that it was through my participation in these groups that I first met the woman who, more than anyone else, has given me a sense that my existence had a point and a mature purpose, merely by her decision to attach herself to it; however fleeting – or, perhaps better, impermanent – this attachment of hers might yet prove to be. This simple decision of hers far outstrips the achievements of all the other claimants which I have eagerly sought out at one time or other, in my often rather frenetic attempts to imbue my life with some sort of valuable meaning. And these secondary attempts, I am sorry to say, do definitely include the Movement itself. That is usually how it happens, is it not? She means even more to me than the great cause does which managed to bring us together. To me that must be a large part of what it is that makes the cause great at all.

Never shall I forget the first moment when I set eyes on her. However, I shall never share my memories of this first, unutterable splendour with anyone else either. A few days later, I happened to notice – no, wait a moment; I am getting myself badly mixed up here. What was it? There was a definite sequence of events. Ah yes. Thus it was. We had begun to parade around in our ancient veils and tartan cloaks in an ever more ecstatic manner, describing ever wider and wilder circles. From the gallery came the delirious stamping sound of the women performing the ancient sexual exposure ritual dance – which is shown in public (that is to say, to the rest of us – a select public, representatives of the broader public) only once a year, at midnight five days after one of the solstices. I forget which. Nor am I entirely certain nowadays as to quite what a solstice is – my memory, unlike the value of *pi*, is not what it was – but I feel it would be a mistake to labour too intensely at so purely technical a point. My future wife, you may suppose, was one of these stamping, skirt-flapping maenads. Not so. Far from it. Had she been such a person, I am quite certain I would not have dared to approach her. Nor, indeed, I very much suspect, would I even have wanted to. Be my attitude in this matter old-fashioned or not, a willingness to expose herself in public is not something I have ever much looked out for in my life companions. It never has been.

No. The truth is somewhat different. The fact is that I was so energetic in my exertions on behalf of the move-ment, and so intent on the ancient Celtic perfection of the knots and arcs of my trajectory, that I failed to pay sufficient attention to the practical limitations of the building which housed us. The simple truth to be borne in mind is we were not our ancestors, bravely expressing our artistic and social needs in the endless fields of our incomparable land, safe and exultant under the open and welcoming air. Far from it. Thus it was that, unbeknownst to myself, I had, in the trance-like enthusiasm of my application, danced my way out of a side-door which had been left open for a reason which no-one subsequently ever cleared up to my satisfaction. Dark hints of infiltra-tion were dropped; but I feel that my ignorance here is such that I cannot add very much to the debate on this particular, troubled and troubling point.

It matters little. I suppose I must have noticed a change in the light values, and I certainly did become aware of a fresh breeze on my face – but, even here, I kept my eyes shut, and I must simply have assumed, what with the fresh air and the sudden access of noise, that I had entered some sort of blissful altered state, and that I was now freely communing with the spirits of my ancestors. And who is to say, with utter certainty, that I am wrong? Air is very frequently associated with uncanny forms of com-munication. We cannot see it, but it produces an effect.

Therefore, so we suppose, perhaps other entities which we cannot see – because they are wholly imaginary – can likewise produce real effects in our present lives. Unlike air, these entities cannot be caught in jars.

Nonetheless, be that as it may, the next thing I knew was that I was being extricated by solicitous hands from a most inadvisable position more or less between the front wheels of a corporation cleaning cart with a picture of a vulture on its side. Soon afterwards, I woke up in a hospital bed, to find myself looking at a nurse who was gazing down at me with one of the most beautiful, kindly, seraphic, fine-cheekboned smiles I had ever seen before or have ever seen since. In fact, she turned out to be virtually a sexual psychopath and was a person to be avoided at all costs, but the sequence of events which brought me to be married unfolded with rigorous inter-locking precision from then onwards.

A week or so after I had left hospital, I saw this same nurse approaching me in a predatory fashion in the main street. To avoid her, I was forced to duck down a curving lane which I had hitherto had no intention whatever of entering. Here I met a young woman with a lisp from the Indian sub-continent – as indeed was she herself. In fact, I actually bumped into her. She asked to be directed to a particular building which was not very far away, but which it was distinctly difficult either for the ignorant to reach, or for the informed to explain the position of without the benefit of copious hand signals, recapitula-tions, scratchings of the head, and hurried sketching of irregular turns. I therefore simply cut through the knot by taking her right to its doors in person.

These doors she went through on her own, after only the most token acknowledgement to me of the consider-able trouble I had just taken on her behalf. I concluded that she feared I had been so painstaking solely because I had had some sort of ulterior motive vis-à-vis the delights of her body. Talk about flattering yourself! If so, she was painfully mistaken; even if not quite one hundred per cent so. However, I decided to let her proceed on this ego-boosting if mildly threatening misreading of the situation, rather than shout out after her that she was profoundly in error. As I myself was turning to leave the vicinity, the only woman who has ever truly mattered to me came out of the doors of the same building, looked at me with an expression of obvious contempt, and that was that.

Well, to be honest, it took a good ten years more for me to be able to convince her that I was a worthy recipient of her finest feelings. At the moment, my hope is that I have finally managed to do so. Of course, even that, even if it is so, may not be permanent – not even with regard to the limited human capacity for permanence, I mean – but it will have to do for now. What else could I reasonably ask for? And where else should I go to look for a reasonable answer? I have had the chance. How many more can truly say as much? I am grateful for that. I have had the chance.

A Personal Letter Sent over an Immense Distance

My dear friend, life goes along without you here, of course; but almost unbearably so. Let me tell you what happened to me personally yesterday. It is so little I am ashamed of it. Where dare I start? With this perhaps. You have always been able to read my symbols aright. Better sometimes than I can do myself. Know then that I had a vision of ancient hunters climbing up an eternal stairway. Except that the stairway was not eternal, merely extremely long, too long for any single lifetime to get to the end of. And I myself looked onto the stairway from a rickety, unsafe construction nearby. And they kept moving past. We did not talk. We observed the correct social distinctions. And it seemed to me it would have taken them an hour to get to the top of the stairway. But none of them seemed to know what an hour way. I mean, to know what an hour was. They were, I am forced to admit, remarkably stupid people. Or perhaps they were merely preoccupied. Or perhaps they were simply extremely busy, that is a possibility too, I concede that.

But even an hour can take one, even at a leisured progression, to so many different places in this neck of the woods. Here, for instance. Let me tell you what I have just seen. The water was lapping against its natural retaining wall as it had done presumably for centuries. People watch it do so sometimes, but at the moment no-one is there. Or, if someone is indeed there, it is only a person from more or less a millennium ago. He wanders along by the water, exiled and alone. Or he does not do so. If people run by a century later, what is it to him? What is it, indeed, to the river? It is hard to influence a river except by falling into it, and even then you could not honestly be said to have caught its attention entirely. But perhaps that small person will cause the fall of an immense empire anyway? Even our own empire, perhaps? Quite possibly we are talking about a female here. Oh, it always so difficult to predict these things! I hope to see you again in time for the Four Little Virgins Festival in the West-North-West Temple-Tower district of the Capital. Once again we shall try to force time to do our bidding. I shall bring the cucumbers. All that I require of you is that you bring yourself and your laugh. And, of course, the sponges.

A Scholarly Life

The old scholar sat in the library day after day at his self-appointed task, working away at his books. Usually they were the same books; although sometimes a particularly satellite-like point required the unearthing of further tomes. Elsewhere in the building, other scholars ignored the whispering and giggling schoolgirls as best they could, if in fact they wanted to, or at least pretended to ignore them as they worked away at their own tasks, whether vital or tedious, important or hopelessly eccentric. He rarely exchanged so much as a word with any of them; and even these few words hardly ever led to even the hint of anything further. To be quite honest, he didn't even like them very much.

Then the war came, and eventually a chance bomb landed a direct hit on the building. It had continued, indomitably, unwilling to be affected by mere politics, and so there were many casualties. Nonetheless, the old scholar continued to work away in the debris. Gradually they reconstructed the building around him and all was well again until, some fifteen years later, an unsuspected, cracked gas main ignited, once again causing massive damage. Many books were lost. Some people too. Fortunately, the old scholar had more or less memorised those few volumes which were absolutely central to his preoccupations. The others he took the opportunity to replace with more modern treatments of the requisite subjects, feeling the need to give back a little of what he had hitherto merely taken.

Three or four years later, after the damage had been repaired as far as was possible, a juvenile maniac ran amok in the main reading-hall, firing off at random at the people sitting there, who were staring at books, often in great dismay, or were sheltering from the cold and the rain. Several were killed. This he did in order to protest at society's selectively callous treatment of poultry, about which he, understandably, felt very passionate. And certainly some of these birds are cooped up terribly. When the lunatic had at last been pacified, the old scholar, by now rather arthritic, re-emerged from under the table with some difficulty, and once more set himself stoically to his task. If he was alone; if a librarian was inadvertently showing an attractive bare leg directly in front of him; if some gamey down-and-out was sitting, sniffing, directly opposite him; if a posse of schoolgirls or schoolboys were swirling around in his field of vision, prancing and shouting, it made no difference whatever to him. He knew what he had to do, and he was intent on doing it. No-one else would ever do it, of that much he was certain.

Then one morning as he was walking to work in the library, a thought suddenly struck him, an insight which had been scraping away somewhere for months before catastrophically breaking through into consciousness, and he realised that his entire work up until that date was thoroughly flawed, misconceived, fatally in error at the very root, and that the masterly summation which he had planned could probably not now be written by him in good faith. Nor was he willing to lie. So it was that, although he had actually reached the fine dark wood of the tall outermost doors of the building, he simply abandoned his task on the instant, in his confusion, and went on walking straight ahead. Within ten minutes he had reached a part of the city which he had never seen before in his entire life.

He felt confused and frightened. What now? He saw at his side the window of a shop which seemed to be selling miscellaneous bricabrac. Did people do this? Every day? Why? Among the items featured there were an oboe; a small hat; a figure from classical antiquity who had a beautifully feminine hairstyle and whose bottom you would very probably be able to see, round behind her, if you were right inside the shop; and a rather shabby knife which was evidently still capable of being put to innumerable helpful uses.

He felt little interest in the oboe – little enough, indeed, to assume that it was a saxophone, for he did not quite know what a saxophone looked like either; but the word 'saxophone' occurred to him on an inspiration as he was gazing into the window-display, and it fully convinced him by its obvious aptness. Also, he was fairly sure he already had a hat at home which, as far as he could remember, was virtually identical to the one on display. He had put it into a cupboard many years before, as being a bit too young and flashy for the latest developments of his taste, and he had forgotten to take it out since. He made a mental note to look it out when he got home, and perhaps even start wearing it again. Life, and so forth. Why not match his clothing to his change of circumstances all round?

He did, however, think that it might be a good idea to go in and buy the knife. Accordingly, he at once disappeared into the shop. And from this moment onwards his actions followed a sadly predictable course. Let us add only that, an hour or so later, an ambulance and a police car drew up outside the shop virtually together. This is hardly likely to be a coincidence. The rest, I think, more or less indicates itself. It would surely be quite unnecessary to linger over it further.

An Admirable Sense of Proportion

W hat was happening? Nothing much. I was just standing there, looking out the window for what I was sure would be the last time. I was doing my best to drink it all in, everything I could see; to make the most of this final opportunity. It had been a wonderful experience. But, all the same, even now, even acting so deliberately, it was obviously impossible somehow to transfer what was out there piece by piece into the memory, for a later total reconstruction. It was too difficult. Or there just wasn't space. Clearly, a lot was going to have to fade or be missed out anyway.

There, still there, was that fine facade of a private building directly opposite, which I think had been turned into an educational institution of some sort. What a stroke of luck, to have had that to admire every time I chose or happened to glance out of the window of my room! And yet, even so, I very soon began to take it for granted. Just at this moment, something was happening there. I watched a group of three elderly people, two men and a woman, make their way slowly down the front steps. Any slip could certainly have had serious consequences. Evidently they were going to be staying here or hereabouts for at least a bit longer, I thought – rather self-pityingly; and, as I now realise, rather presumptively – for they, or any one of them, or any pair of them, could have been leaving for the other end of the world right at that very moment.

I shouldn't have been seeing that. Not from this angle anyway. It was two minutes since the summons of a knock at the door, or perhaps the ring of the telephone, ought officially to have called me away. It would have to happen very soon now. How casually the three talked among themselves, all the same; taking so much for granted, already shared between them, already known. They got to the foot of the steps and stood there, evidently waiting for something.

Something moving right below the window also caught my gaze. It turned out to be a boy reading a magazine of some kind; perhaps it was a comic. Certainly it was glossy and illustrated. He walked in a kind of swaying way, now halting, now moving on, as the contents of what he was reading made renewed demands or released what had been their fiercest grip on his attention. Presumably the elderly trio must have seen him too; or his presence had somehow registered on their various powers of vision, a detail of the view (unlike me), assuming them all still to *have* adequate powers of vision. Which they seemed to have. Not that they did anything about it. What could they do? What ought they to do? The situation called for nothing; and that seemed to be pretty well what they were giving it. An admirable sense of proportion, all things told. Passers-by are usually just passers-by.

Just then, among the trees opposite, on a higher street up the slope, a smartly dressed young woman walked swiftly by. I saw her for a few seconds as she passed in front of a low wall and a gateway before she reached the next building, which hid her. I am certain none of the other four saw her. The boy could not have seen her; though I suppose she might in real life have been his elder and devoted sister, for all I knew. But for some reason I felt at once that they were both easy inhabitants of this large city, that they always had been, and that they probably always would be until their separate groups of grieving children wished them a heartbroken farewell; and that, even so, they would probably never come any closer to each other than this. And even if they did, they would never know about this. About what? About this. It's not very much, is it? It's hardly even worth talking about, I suppose. Still. You make your own choices. For all I know, in ten years' time they'll get married to each other. A few seconds after that there was a gentle knock at my door.

An Idyll

How amazing to wake up there and to see the bright sunlight flood through the flimsy curtains, over the walls, the bed, the cheap but quite serviceable furniture. It looked almost like the same sunlight that you might see anywhere. She was still asleep. All her aggression seemed to leave her when she was sleeping – though I can't tell what sort of dreams she might have been having. Not that I mean to suggest she was aggressive all the time. Still. Every so often some of it came out. The room, however, had been made as personal as she could make it, but in some moods it seemed like a fairly doomed struggle against the sheer triumphant crudity and inhuman bluntness of the prefabricated architecture which contained it.

As it turned out, though it took her a while to concede this, she lived in what must have been one of the ugliest and most extensive areas of brutal modernist housing in the entire city. At first she still felt the need to profess great loyalty to it. Perhaps she had lived there too long not to. I had never been there before in my entire life. Well, why should I have been? Why go looking for trouble? I had enough problems of my own already. It was not what she would have chosen given a free hand, obviously, she kept saying, but I had to take what was offered or I would end up with nothing and it could have been worse. Much worse. With a bit of luck I won't be here for long. But she had already been there for well over three years. Nearer four years.

Quietly I forced my way out of bed and went over to the window. Actually, once my feet were on the carpet, it required only two more steps to get there, and they were not particularly long steps either. Little was happening on the street immediately outside; but a bigger street could be seen beyond the houses opposite, and here there was already a fair amount of traffic in action and people in slow, dogged movement. Who are all these people, who have to be out there already getting somewhere at seven o'clock in the morning? I knew I could do with thinking about that, and that it wouldn't really take much thinking about either; but I decided to postpone this painful operation for as long as possible. There were other moods to revel in.

I could see how ugly and loveless and inelegant the houses opposite were. And the buildings of a slightly different design which I could see beyond and over them – though design is surely too strong a word for what seemed to amount to little more than merely turning an oblong box over on its end. The sunlight did something for their grimness, but they nonetheless remained grim. Who would have loitered here? Who would have chosen to be here? And all at once it occurred to me that I was in one room in exactly the same sort of ugly building myself. Who would so much as want to give it a second glance? Or even a first one. But how uncanny and magical it felt all the same. And for some reason the whole thing suddenly seemed so hopeful. What if all the other rooms hereabouts had interiors like this? Why should they not have? Of course they did! As if, no matter how hard we might try to do so, we could in fact never quite manage to get it completely wrong.

Perhaps it needs a little more. Does it need a little more? Very well: I'll give just a little more. How about this? And so it went on until one day her husband turned up most unexpectedly when he ought to have been in London and did his best to kick the shit out of me.

An Ordinary Close of Day

It was evening. The sun had very recently set. But all was as it should be, the offerings had been made, the prayers had been prayed. There was therefore no doubt that the Father of All Things would be putting in a renewed appearance on the following day. And it was then, or about then, that Karttata-Farnara-Wara came out of the tent and strolled a few paces forward towards the wood. He was going nowhere in particular. More than anything he was simply enjoying the cool air all around him. He looked up. The sky was clear. The immense flock of birds which had filled the heavens for almost the entire day since just before sunrise had finally flown completely by. Miraculous. He had known a few longer visitations even in the past five or so years. Everything was peaceful. The other men would no doubt be out soon, those of them who would choose to do so at all. As far as they could tell, there were no enemies very near. Perhaps, with luck, with the guidance of the Great God Ttatan, the enemies were all across the river fighting each other and would weaken themselves so much that his own tribe would itself be able to cross later and make substantial advances over the land which should by rights be theirs.

Old crimes would eventually be paid for – there was no fear of that not happening. It had to happen. It was plaited within the ordering of things by the beings who ruled. A few birds rustled nearby. A few sounds of children briefly yelling, or of distant laughter, or of eating utensils being used reached him as he stood there, breathing in the scent of aromatic grasses, deep in thought. He could hear virtually anything that was happening nearby. He could hear so much. So overwhelmingly much. Of course, there were limits even to his extraordinary range. For instance, he did not hear one particular set of feet thud as they landed significantly in mud far off, at a water's edge, the first of them all to do so; and a great cry go up, and shouts of praise to a strange murdered God whom he had never heard of, that they had reached their place of sanctuary in safety, that the worst was past for them, that the tide had turned at last, and that all was now theirs. That they could now set out and conquer, claiming all that they found for their righteous possession. But how could he possibly have heard it? It was happening several days journey away, at the far coast of the continent, where at the moment it was still an intensely bright day.

Horror Story

After a while, I realised that something was indeed wrong with the car. It had stopped moving. I looked around me. It seemed as if almost everything else had stopped moving too. Then I saw something happening between the railings of the necropolis which I happened to have halted or stalled beside – or whatever it was that I had just done. We had had an argument, needless to say. There is no other way in which I can describe it. Any other way is inadequate. Anyway, what I saw then was this. In the early evening, pensively, the ghosts were emerging from their graves. Without waiting for the word of command, they seeped unanimously towards the nearby road which would take them to the centre of the town – a town which most of them had presumably known in life. It was still a journey of a good few minutes – although obviously to some extent this would depend on what was the maximum speed they would be able to reach. I dare say no-one really knows these things. They had crossed (who knows how?) the boundary of the cemetery and they had begun to flood forward beneath a street-lamp, a strange unruly mass of unequal visitants – when one of those at the front of the group hesitated and stopped.

What? What was that thing moving down there at the base of a low wall just behind the lamp-standard? Lamp-standard? Lamp-post, surely. Anyway, an unearthly shriek rang out, in a numinous sort of way. It was a rat! A rat! At once the crowd of ghosts disappeared, as if a single shout or puff of air had extinguished them. An amazing response to such a trivial eruption, I would have thought. Well, I did think so. I was nearly there at the time. Nonetheless, the rat sauntered about for a while, and then vanished nonchalantly into a suburban garden. Then, shortly afterwards, the snow began to fall for the first time that year. A dog emerged, rounding the corner at a run, followed by a young man eagerly trying to keep up with it. One of these mammals was myself, but I don't want to accord that more importance than it deserves. They were good times, all in all. I wish I could remember them more often than I do.

From Another Sacred Book

And he said to them, Listen. It is important to behave decently. You should try to be good. We all should. And they replied, Master, we know that pretty well already. This is a very long way to come, and a hard way over near impossible roads particularly at this time of the year, only for us to hear this. Or for us to hear only that. We grow faint from apprehension. Our enemies will sneer at us and taunt us. Well, you have seen them yourself. You have heard them, have you not? They do so already. In fact, to be quite frank, at times they seem to do little else. Tell us then a mightier information. Something which lies and which must lie immensely beyond our power to understand. Challenge us. Humiliate us. Laugh at us. Despise us. Make it all worthwhile somehow. We feel ourselves sadly oppressed by all these tiny truths.

So he thought for a moment, and laughed heartily, yea, until the tears came into his eyes. Which is the only time in his whole sorry life that he was ever observed to laugh, apart perhaps from the occasion when he chanced upon a picture of the expression on the face of the last of the ultra-orthodox. And he said to them, such trust deserves what I intend to repay it with. Listen then to this. And he spoke to them as follows.

Now, there was a man there who came from Xnukk, which in our language is Portobello, and his name was Tiberius Paunce-Gonad, and he was one of the Portobello Paunce-Gonads; and he was gay. As was his wife and as were his three sons; and his five daughters were gay also. Everyone was gay, in fact. For it was a feast day.

And he did something, I forget quite what it was, but it was so terrible whatever it was that it caused him to deserve to be carefully reconstructed from the scattered fragments after he had died in order to be personally tortured for ever and ever and ever and ever and so on and for nearly twice as much. (So that after, say, five hundred and twenty-three million years of excruciating agony, and having boiling water poured down his throat and red-hot pokers run up his arsehole and so forth – suitably reinforced for the purpose – I refer here, of course, to his arsehole – or whatever the immaterial or spiritual equivalent of that is; for, seeking as we are to express the totally impossible, we are forced to speak merely in striking images which must carry the conviction which the concepts behind them cannot – so that even after such a half eternity it could hardly be said even to be beginning, the pain, even after so long an interval, since it was eternal and ever lasting and was never a second further away from its starting-point no matter for how long it had continued. Have you all got that copied down all right?) Where was I? Something like: tortured by the all-kind and all-powerful being who had made him as he was, with his abilities and his lack of them, and who had hardened his heart against the gift of grace, which he freely offers even to those whom he has so constructed as to be unable to accept it, which he well knows, for nothing can be done that is done without him. Amen. Is that clear enough for you?

And Tiberius, in a moment of unusual boldness, cried out to the Great Maker: Lord, if you didn't like me so much, why did you bother to make me this way in the first place? It's you who did it, after all. Even my ability to choose for myself, such as it is, is only the ability which you fitted me out with at the start. Why blame me? Make me a better person, and then set me what trials you will. For with thy grace and mercy I would have triumphed over those trials. Why make me one way and then send me trials which you know perfectly well I will not be so constituted by you as to be able to overcome? This infinite kindness of yours seems to be very like a sort of cruelty which is sadly familiar to me.

For He who made it all made all of it; and if millions have squirmed and failed to make sense of how their supposed or known freedom can co-exist with this total fabrication, their failure does not demonstrate the existence of some great truth which lies beyond sense, since truth in the first instance must make sense to those who speak the language in which the words are expressed. For otherwise how can it be known to be truth? How can it be true, if it in fact expresses nothing but uncertainty. No. Though such is how they flatter themselves, their words fail to make mere sense, and the only known form of sense there is, simply because they are in fact expressing nonsense. What do you think of that?

And the Lord replied, Shut up and suffer, Tiberius. That is obviously what I made you for. It is not for you to question me. All are worms, but you are a worm particularly. Any questions?

Fate

He rode in under the archway, and reached a small, busy square. Here he stopped and looked around. Although many eyes had clocked his arrival, it seemed to him that he had somehow turned up among them virtually unobserved. For a moment he even wondered whether he in fact were not actually somewhere else; but he dismissed this idea as being implicitly unworthy of further scrutiny. He was certainly here. At length he espied a promising figure reclining under an awning in a far corner, evidently entirely at his ease, and he steered his way towards him as deftly as he could between the tottering heaps of breads and baskets and vegetables.

'Edjer vitize?' he asked amicably. The other spat out the weed he was languorously chewing, wiped his mouth with his sleeve, and eventually deigned to look up at the mounted figure who had thus addressed him.

'What language is that, stranger?' he enquired with no great appearance of caring much one way or the other. 'It's a polyglot civilisation, I grant you. But even so. That isn't one of the languages we use here in this town, is it?'

'Evidently,' replied the stranger, 'I have travelled further than I thought. I wonder can you help me? I am looking for the source of an unparalleled phenomenon.'

'Who isn't? And which phenomenon might that be, Mac?' replied the unimpressed, prone native. 'We get quite a lot of them around these parts, and that I can tell you free of charge, gratis and for nothing. Yes, sir, in all three of those ways which I have just adumbrated. Zippedeedoodah. A prayer, sir; a mere prayer.'

'I see. I wonder. Are you by any chance a homosexual?' asked the stranger.

'What? Why do you say that? I refute the accusation thus. Drunk, perhaps; drugged possibly; but that is absolutely all. I think you will find that most of the people here are drugged anyway. Now tell me what you want to know or I'll get the soldiers to flay you alive and sell tickets to some rich local perverts for a ringside seat at the experiment. Don't think I wouldn't, Pileface. How else do you think I got to be so rich in the first place?'

'I hasten to comply with your wishes,' said the traveller. 'Let me explain a little. I am an expert in the doings of the heavens. Rarely does an immensity body out or ejaculate up there but that my eye is upon it, able to follow through whichever circumjacencies it eventrates itself until it should finally and in triumph impinge on the sterticulate of my imfuscolutions. All right so far?'

'It pleases you to say so,' said the lolling native. 'Do by all means go on, if you must. It is not the first time I have heard such stories in my lifetime.'

'Certes, Master. There appeared in the empyrean an inflammatory obtrudescence, which by some is yclepped a sort of arrow, but also as a star, look you, which appeared to point at one part of the horizon, as viewed from my study window. Crund, thought I. This is it. The signal is come at last. I must perforce follow it. And follow it I did. Therefore am I here. Ostensibly, at least.'

'You saw something in the night sky which told you to come to this shithole, is that right?' asked the local, suddenly alert and alive to numerous advantageous future possibilities which at once scintillated in his raddled, mercantile brain.

'Querstaq fnah, jimm. Though not exactly to here, perhaps. I also had a vision. There is, I believe, a small hovel in the vicinity with a strange tripartite erection adjunct to its roof. Do you know of it? It is thither I would go. That is the exactness of the sought place. I shall liberally reward you with figs, money and empty promises if you will only instruct me how to find this vapance, or even only the airt to this ort.'

'Hmm. I see. In other words, it sounds to me very like the same old story. Right. First, please let me tell you two things. The second of which is that either you or your horse is smelling particularly rank after your journey. Harsh, but necessary. The first was something about women leaping around waving tambourines, which I find I now cannot exactly remember. No matter. The fact is you do not master the language totally, oh stranger. Nor do you, I fear, entirely master the vocabulary of the night sky. For the erection which you seek, I am sorry to say, disappeared several years ago. Night passed, and morning came, and it had succumbed to the subsidence which is endemic in these parts. Thou art, in short, too late, Boss. And you can keep the figs.'

At which the traveller started and said, 'I do not think so.' And, holding out a purse stuffed with almost silver, he said: 'This is for you, friend, if you tell me you know where the house which I have just described is to be found.'

'Of course I know where it is to be found,' said the mendacious layabout. 'Everyone in this town knows. It is up on the hill behind us, and a dirt track which many of us know of will easily take you there. Look: that white spot up there is on it. Possibly it is a goat. Or perhaps a head.'

Well satisfied, the traveller threw the purse down to the oaf on the ground. 'Well have you spoken,' he said, 'oaf. Now tell me how I am to find this track and an equal to this shall also be yours for your trivial and graceless service.'

'Look,' said the guide. 'This is of course entirely up to you, effendi. But tell me this. Do you really, at your time of life, want to go gallivanting about up scrub-lined hill-sides – and all in search of what? Do thyself a favour, sunshine. Listen to me.'

'I am listening,' said the searcher. 'What do you suggest?'

'Look,' said the first, 'I may be only an old pervert, depending on whether you think forty-five is old or not, but I think I know what you'll enjoy a lot better than that. What is it you expect to find up there anyway?'

'I shall tell you. I am surprised you do not know already. I truly expect to find the answer to all my questions. I shall find there all that the spirit of man has ever sought for. For there, I know it even in my bones, is at last come to light the culminating moment not merely of my existence or of yours, but of all existence as such. And I shall go there and embrace it with all my powers and learn from it more than I had ever thought it possible to know. Is that what you wished to learn from me?'

'Indeed it is,' said the transformed fish. 'And it is pretty much as I had expected. Look. Let me explain something to you. For merely a hundred times what you have already given me – how could I in fairness accept less? – even for so trifling a sum I would gladly allow you to go through that door behind me, that beaded and entrancingly winking entrance which you have rarely been able to keep your gaze off for long. And rightly too, if I may say so.'

'But why on earth', asked the astonished wayfarer, 'should I ever want to do that? It is the purpose and meaning of life I seek, nothing else, nothing lesser. I have not travelled so far merely to experience realistic pleasures.'

'As I was saying, Master,' said the genie. 'Listen. It is my doorway. It leads to a stairway up to the windows behind that balcony up there. See? All right. Now, in there at present, to the best of my recollection, are a couple of my daughters, a couple of *their* daughters, my wife, and, unless I am mistaken, her mother too, who is actually a very attractive woman in a mildly terrifying sort of way. Needless to say, as is the custom of the country hereabouts, all of them are sexually available at my say-so. I don't mind. I have other pleasures. Now. What do you say? Stay there as long as you like. Adopt my name and liabilities if it pleases you. By all means bounce about on the floor or in a hammock with all of them at once. Of course, you would have to use a very large hammock. Still: what of that? We *have* a very large hammock. What do you say? We've had people pass this way before, you know. And, if you want to know the truth, I reckon they have always been diminished by the experience that awaits them up in the oddly alluring hovel on that hill over there. It is, I am forced to suggest, inevitably shot through with a significant and inescapable degree of existential fraudulence. What do you say?' And to end this sorry tale he also added a catalogue of disgraceful and scarcely believable sexual suggestions such as I can in no way repeat here. It took him at least ten more minutes to do so.

When he had finished, the bemused traveller wrestled

107

with his feelings for a long while, and then triumphantly cried out: 'Jerribfasset! Kwad!' And so it was. He had made his choice. Nor did he regret it for a moment – not even when the time came for him to be led away from wherever exactly it was he ended up in by the grinning local police. How could it have been otherwise? You cannot escape your destiny. Nor can you easily escape someone else's. And now, if you'll excuse me, I must nip out before they catch me. Thank you again.

Live and Let Live

I had, of course, intended to explore the entire town, as far as I could, during my stay there, but I knew that this was going to last for a whole month, slightly over a month in fact, and so I felt myself to be under no compulsion to leave the flat and go searching for visual treasures at once. It was, moreover, such a pleasant flat. Such a delightful improvement on what I had been used to back home. There was also free access to a little balcony that came with it. Or perhaps it was not quite so little a balcony. The fact is it ran along outside the house, three storeys high, from one retaining wall to the next, and was thus as broad as the whole room beyond it. Furthermore, the wall and railings and plants were so arranged that, when one was out there, admiring the busy square below, and the small line of impressive shops, and the passers-by on the other side of the street, and occasional glimpses of people at the window opposite, one felt oneself to be invisible. Nor was this entirely an illusion. Very few could possibly know that one was there. Not unless they had enlisted techno-logical aid – and why would anyone want to do that? It was hardly worth sweeping with binoculars so unpromis-ing a target. Thus it was that after some twenty-six or twenty-seven days there I had still not ventured out to explore much beyond the very conveniently sited supermarket just round the corner at the near end of the street. I may even have been developing a secret reputation as a mysterious foreign recluse. I don't know. I talked to practically no-one. There was also the language problem. However, all that changed on the day when I was treacherously thrown off the balcony. Alas, the fall killed me outright, so, obviously, I am unable to discuss the matter any further. Perhaps the local police will be able to help you in this connection, should you particularly wish to pursue it. But I have to say I suppose this to be most unlikely. They never seemed to be particularly interested, for some reason or other. Still, it was a beautiful balcony, and I feel privileged to have been allowed to enjoy it for as long as I did. I always felt safe there. I can't pretend I didn't. I had no reason to believe that anyone else had keys to the apartment. Except for the owner, of course. Which stands to reason. One could hardly expect it to be arranged otherwise. Perhaps no-one else had done it. As for the accident – which was certainly no accident – I regret to say I was unable to see who did it. Really and truly. I am not trying to protect anyone. I am certainly not lying. I heard something, I admit that. But it was quite an active street down below. I was always hearing things when I was there. And as for the neighbours. Well, I'll say nothing about them. Live and let live, and so forth. I certainly heard no-one approaching – not until it was too late anyway. I suppose my body could have lain up there unnoticed on the balcony for long enough. Perhaps the owner will have discovered it. Or the next lessee. I hope the smell did not give away its presence. Or was I thrown off the balcony? No; on second thoughts, I don't think I was. I was *left* on the balcony for dead, that is what happened. Yes. That's it. I had been struck treacherously on the back of the head. I don't know quite why I claimed earlier to have been thrown off. A natural weakness for melodrama, I suppose. But I got up about an hour or so later, after the assault (not yet dead, of course) and I wandered back into the house. I could not help noticing that the communicating door was slightly ajar. I think that must have been what happened. Something like that. Yes. Then, dazed, I think I wandered back out onto the balcony. And it was at that point that I fell over. Or something like that. Yes. That gets it all down. That is the broad outline of the course of events. I was always more one for the broad outline than for the minutiae of the details. Ask anyone. They'll tell you. I still had a few days due to me that I had already paid for. Still; not to worry. I don't suppose that'll make too much difference now. I suppose it was motiveless. The outrage. Perhaps it wasn't. If not then theft, probably. One can't be expected to know everything, after all. So: not an unalleviated success. A greater success than what I had anticipated, certainly; but not without certain drawbacks. It would be pointless to close one's eyes to the obvious truth of that. A considerable, but not an unalleviated success. That is fair, I think. One tries to be fair. I sometimes think it is more important to be fair than almost anything else. Ah well. What else can I be expected to do now? Oh look! There's my return ticket.

Something Trickling Out Of Somewhere

This afternoon, among a pile of books, in an untidy
shop at the end of a lane, which I often visit in the
afternoons and evenings, I unearth, of all things, an
illustrated guide to a museum in Cologne. It is being
offered for fifty pence, the cheapest possible price.

The thing is, I remember actually visiting that museum.
I cannot remember how often. More than once, I am
fairly certain, during a stay of a couple of weeks at an
aunt's house about forty minutes away by a clean, modern, efficient train. She is long dead. That was twenty-one
years ago. Or, now I think about it again, say twenty years
and a half. I was twenty-three years old. One could also
say, nearly twenty-three and a half.

I remember sitting in a cafe in the building, alone and
lonely. There were a couple of people at a nearby table,
but the place was very quiet. I remember a bored guard
involving me in conversation, about the danger of standing too near the pictures, and spoiling them with my
breath. When he heard my foreign accent, his attitude at
once became slightly more formal.

Now I sit in a little room which I had never seen then;
which I would move into at the end of the year following;

and where I have been for almost twenty years. Well: for not quite nineteen and a half. I flick through the pictures. I can even remember actually looking at a few of the things themselves: the disappointing Friedrichs, the Rembrandt self-portrait, which would not say as much to me as I was willing it to say. I still remember the clean, bright room; the travelling exhibition of what seemed to me even then to be dreadful modern American art; the young women who seemed to be everywhere, with all their different lives in front of them.

Did I see that striking Edvard Munch there? I suppose I must have done. I don't remember it. As it happens, I remember some of his photographs – little ordinary snapshots, but very powerful – in a large gallery in Edinburgh three or four or five years ago. When? I don't remember. But that at least must be a matter of public record anyway. Not for the first time I thought that a reasonably authentic record of something actual was worth more than most artistic fabrications; that in a photograph of an artist's studio the works of his that one can see, that are on show, are usually the least interesting and significant part of the image in question.

This very book, still looking impressively new and undamaged by time or anything else, must already have been almost a decade old when I was wandering through that building looking at the Munch photographs. There is a rather attractive, airy photograph of the building on the front cover. I do not remember this in the slightest, even though I have been there. I do remember passing a bright, gay fountain on my way there. I vaguely remember the groups of people I passed. I remember that it seemed as if it was all happening now, and it all had to be happening now.

I dare say that was true, as far as it went. Now I throw

114

the book down onto the bed beside the word-processor. There is also a cap there; there are a few disposable razors; there is a grey plastic bag, for I bought new shoes yesterday; and there is a phone-card. I am slightly disappointed that a certain person I know has not phoned me this evening. When I left that building there were still years to go before I would meet her. Not that one is ever quite aware of that at the time, needless to say. Still, there are well over three hours of the day left – nearly four – and innumerable things are no doubt still possible. That is usually the case anyway.

A Life's Work

Here you are. In at last, safe, out of the filthy rain; the incipient, depressing darkness; something else that needed to be struggled against and overcome. And it was struggled against and overcome; you were successful in that too. The home; the light; the warmth. No-one else there yet, true; but even the silence is somehow welcoming after all the wetness and noise and gloom and sullen passage. There is already a friendly heat in the place, and a single flick brings light to it too. Suddenly, it seems possible that one is living in the right century, and the right country, and the right body, and the right everywhere. Everything seems, just possibly, to be right.

Then on into the front room, picking up something, something no doubt trivial, that was put down at the start of the day. Dropped there, perhaps. These objects whose personalities and history you are familiar with, even those which someone else bought. Other people will arrive soon, one in particular, out of the darkness and the rain, from different buildings, where for one reason or another they are forced to spend so much of their time apart from you; from different bodies too, you might say; and every-

117

thing will be as nearly all right as possible again for as long as it is going to be. Great. This is it.

Or perhaps someone else is already there, unknown. Most unlikely. Yet that too is possible, I suppose. Is there a motive? Mere theft, perhaps? That's none too probable. A sliding or swishing sound; something against the skull or the back of the head, which may even be too sudden for pain. Out of it into nothing. Right away. Suspecting nothing.

Instantaneously right out of it. Nothing more. A noise, and several objects on the carpet. Rain is still falling, and there are plenty of problems, but only for others. The ones who are still approaching this treasured place, for instance. And even though once they may have been dear to you, they are dear to you no longer. The next turn of the light-switch, whoever does it, is not in the slightest a factor in your existence. Even so, it almost certainly doesn't happen, and you very likely turn on the light-switch next yourself. Still waiting; still happy; still hopeful. Or not, as the case may be. Nothing more to be asked for. Just life.

But There is More to Life than the merely Spiritual, Natasha

Ivan Nikolayevitch Fyetukov whizzed through the fresh, bright, reawakened countryside in his spanking new gig. He was on his way to visit Nadyezhda Platonovna, who had lately arrived for the summer at her estate of Anastassianovo, barely half an hour's drive away from his own rather less substantial one if the roads remained fine, and if no overwhelming mishap befell him. All seemed set remarkably fair. Lodka, his magnificent bay gelding, was eating up the versts as if he had not been out on the road for months and were trying to disperse a grim season of frustration and anticipation in one joyous and prolonged bout of speed. True, he persevered in his strange and characteristic travelling motion, holding his aristocratic head remarkably steady as he seemed to scan the horizon, exactly as if he were searching for the lost city of Vitebsk, or for his lost love, which was the sort of ploy that Ivan Nikolayevitch himself had long since given up as a complete waste of time and a blight on the life which continued to need to be lived. If two men joined together at the waist, thought Ivan Nikolayevitch, were in fact a horse in motion, they would certainly be Lodka. Or Lobka, as he had originally been called. He was unsure if the name had decisively been changed, and at what point; and, if so, why. But, no doubt fortunately, there was very little difference between the two. He was a fine horse, whatever his name was. Of that there could be absolutely no doubt.

Other thoughts distracted him from this foray into Natural History – which was the subject he had studied for several years, with no great distinction, at the provincial but still distinguished University of K., under wily old Professor Klopshtok, a Baltic German with a terrible accent and a secret in his past about which he talked to no-one except his pet parrot, Schiller. Every so often, the little brute would interrupt his incommunicative whistles and profanities or brooding silences, to pipe up with a cry of 'Goethe! Goethe!' At which the Professor would often be so convulsed with laughter that at times he would even sink slowly to the carpet, shaking and gasping with mirth, and resting there on the floor for a good twenty minutes or so, perhaps twenty-five, until the spasm had abated. Mad, of course, wholly mad; but then, he was a German. You had to try to bear these things in mind and be fair. Of late, it had crossed Fyetukov or Fetyukov's mind that the Professor may even have welcomed these interruptions and could provoke them from the bird at will (if such it really was) by a secret sign with one of his eyebrows, in order to break up or even end a particularly unrewarding session of tuition. It could not be denied that he was a man capable at times of a great subtlety. Dear old K.! What a wonderful town it could be at times, for all its failings! Which of us did not have failings? And our fathers too.

Nadyezhda Platonovna would soon, he was sure, be his. After all, who else (he asked himself) would particularly want her? The fact is he didn't even particularly want her himself. It was the money and the land that was the main thing, and the exhilarating, inebriating prospect of the end at last to the insecurity which had dogged his entire life so far. This was largely the result of a lackadaisical disposition which he had inherited from a deeply selfish and egotistical father, and it had at one point even forced him to work for his living for quite a few months in Petersburg – eight months, nearly nine; thirty-five weeks minus a mere two days, a Thursday and a Friday – as a mere governmental functionary. Those dreadful days, he was quite sure, would never return now. Surely they could not. How much misfortune was a man to be expected to bear? And there was more. He could not even pretend to himself any longer that he was not, to some extent, noticeably bald.

Nadyezhda Platonovna, he knew perfectly well, was no beauty now and could not possibly ever have been one. She was also highly limited intellectually – especially when compared to the man whom she evidently thought *he* was. He had talked to an intellectual once when in the capital, there could be no doubt about that. A man who had had three books published – and had written a fourth too, which was eaten (his only copy of it, alas!) by his pet spaniel, Digby. But at least she did not have that tiresome and surely nearly always imaginary interest in art and science and that sort of futility which so many plain, rather fat women often possessed. And they then wondered why they could not attract an estimable mate! The answer to that was very obvious, surely. Very obvious indeed. And he himself sometimes wondered at things too. He wondered whether Nadyezhda Platonovna would be as happy to see him as he hoped she would be, and as she had lately seemed to be becoming. Oh yes. As he negotiated at quickening speed a tricky bend, he wondered whether she would be flustered or elated, and to what degree, when she heard his gig rumble and bounce into the yard below her window, and himself not quite fall out, she would stop whatever it was she was doing to run down – which made him wonder, almost forgetful of what else he himself was doing, what it was that she indeed *was* doing just at the moment. Who ever knows these things?

Well, why not? At just that moment Nadyezhda Platonovna moved slightly on the chaise longue on which she was lying. As she did so, her cap fell off. Jerked out of her post-prandial snooze, she raised her head and looked around the room. No-one else there, thank goodness. She re-arranged about her substantial person the smooth, caressing folds of her thin silken gown and then laboriously sat up. Indeed, no-one else was there. Good. 'If only I were a man,' she moaned to herself, 'I could then have become a monk.' She lazily fired off a volley of four or five slow, quiet farts; then she lifted a small golden bell and daintily rang it just the once. It probably cost a fortune, and it gave out a surprisingly penetrating sound.

There was a knock at the door, and she looked up to see which of her domestics had responded. This morning it was Trofim. Or was it perhaps afternoon already? He carried a huge tray on which reposed a magnificent selection of luxurious delicacies, gourmet rarities which only someone to whom cost meant nothing could have had provided for her in such riotous and unnecessary profusion. Having deposited this groaning treasure on the exquisitely detailed table at her side, he bowed yet again, turned, and took his leave with all the considerable grandeur and stateliness that he had shown when first she became aware of him, already a tried and trusted retainer in her family, nearly four decades ago now. Even the trivial degree of nudity which she had insisted on as a quid pro quo for keeping him in service after she had, during that terrible afternoon, found some stolen silver knives in his pocket while she had been standing on top of him, even that seemed at such moments to become him. And by now it was only at such moments, after all, that she had come to insist on it. One had to know where to draw the limits, that was the important thing. One had to know what it was that must nonetheless at all costs be kept a private matter.

After he had left, she locked the door, then picked up the tray herself and moved over to the window. Here she sat down on her favourite seat, admiring the small garden below, and the wall which divided off her own living from the boundless spaces of the level plains beyond. Was there really another continent over there somewhere? How thrilling! How delightful! Then, with her eyes closed, she reached out and picked up at absolute random the first silver vessel that her hand chanced to touch. She nibbled at one or two morsels from within it, before emptying the rest over her stomach and spreading it as evenly as she could up and down her torso. I dare say she has actually taken her gown off by now. Perhaps not. But surely she has? She looked around, saw no-one, and closed her eyes. What could be more relaxing? Ah! The fine details! The final details!

She proceeded to do likewise with four or five other pots and jars, until, very soon, from the neck down, she was entirely covered with rich, rare and desirable food-stuffs. A feast which would exult and sate anyone. Then she lay back, sighing, and lifted her eyes to the clouds. By coincidence, a few minutes later, when she to her own surprise jerked awake again, it should have been at precisely the moment at which the keenly alert Ivan

123

Nikolayevitch ought to have been eagerly guiding Lobka or Lodka through her main gate and across her yard, stopping with a charming suddenness directly in front of the big door, and throwing the whole place into a sudden flurry of reorganisation and sotto voce imprecation.

However, at precisely that moment Ivan Nikolayevitch did not arrive. Nor did he arrive during the next half-hour afterwards. And some time later, when Nadyezhda Platonovna is luxuriously being soaped in her bath, he has still not arrived. This begins almost to get worrying. He can hardly have changed his mind, can he? Surely he could not have met anyone else while travelling along such a rarely frequented road? Puzzling indeed, ladies and gentlemen. Very puzzling. There is little point in denying, ladies and gentlemen, lovers of the west and admirers of the deep soul of the east, that it is all, as usual, an extremely puzzling turn of events.

Classified Information

I had been sitting in the garden for a very long while that afternoon. I think in all I must have been there for more than two hours, perhaps even more than six, before I noticed that there was actually a body lying over by the far wall. This was alarming. This was most alarming, obviously. There could be no two ways about it. This was extremely alarming. I didn't want to have noticed that at all. For one thing, it was not my garden. Of course, I'm not sure exactly what sort of body it was: I was merely staying there for a few weeks in summer, largely thanks to the kind offices of a friend – or, more precisely, of the wife of his boss's brother. This was a complication that I could well have done without. I could be more specific, but why bother? There are some languages which can describe even such complex social relationships in a single word. Perhaps even in a simple word rather like *chongchh*. It wouldn't surprise me, though I am certainly no expert in this field. In fact, I suppose, to be honest, I am in many ways rather ignorant. But what a shock it was, and no mistake.

About four o'clock, I went in for a light snack. Then I looked again at the erotic photographs I had found in their woefully inadequate hiding place the previous day. They were the usual stuff: secret, seductive and charming. It was strange to see such intimate images of a woman one had met only a couple of times, on rather staid, formal occasions, but there we have it. All sorts of pulses must be running beneath all sorts of serious or unpromising surfaces. I stole virtually none of them to add to my collection. It is a very select collection anyway. Certainly I greatly preferred the pictures which showed only her, often more or less sitting beside a window which I myself used to sit beside, perhaps even a few years before, to those which also showed indications of the presence or the person of the husband. Of course, it was their house. It was theirs to do with it whatever they liked. I was not their judge. Still, I couldn't help to some degree judging them. I suppose I judged them not proven. To me it seemed to be the fairest decision under the circumstances, although I suppose, as usual, there will be those who think such a decision fairly reeks of cowardice. Perhaps it does. Who cares? I couldn't care less, actually.

Anyway, I have no reason to believe that it wasn't their house. I went out in the early evening and I sat down in the last of the major warmth of the day. When I eventually could bring myself to look over, I saw that the body had disappeared. Quite gone. I could see no marks either from where I was sitting. That was a relief, at least. It was certainly not the sort of problem that I wanted to be forced to deal with myself. I don't even really belong to this neighbourhood. Let them sort out their own problems, for heaven's sake. I have enough of my own. It wasn't a drug-induced vision – that's one thing I think we ought to be clear about. What did I do next? Ah yes; I remember. I sat there, flicking for a while through another publication which I had also found in the house, but which I feel it would be too hazardous even to risk naming here and now. I had just happened to find it, that was all. Down behind a cushion while I was looking for something else. I felt a sort of profound sociological interest in the contents, that is all. I would say it was all comparatively innocent. Anyway, when eventually I lost interest in that after a couple of hours or so, I set to reading a little more of, I suppose, what was a far worthier book which I had picked up off the bookcase by the bed. It was one of the great European classics. In fact, it seemed to be more than one of them at once. You know the sort of thing, I trust?

'Now, the entire country was full of those who were ill and crippled and sick in the head, and people who would believe more or less anything that told them what they wanted to hear. And he told them what they wanted to hear. And he was able to make a living.' That sort of thing. I don't think I stayed with this one for terribly long. From a nearby house, over a garden somewhere, I could hear the sound of someone's distant but not sufficiently distant television. As far as I could make out, the voice on it was saying: 'It's Maurizio Ftumsh. It's half past sex. It's time to urinate.' I tried to ignore it as best I could. At least I had just learned what the proper time was, sort of. Not that I had particularly wanted to know. Still, I knew. That was something.

History

It was agreed that the conspirators were to assemble at the great tower nearest to the centre of the city at midnight. To be as inconspicuous as possible, they were to make their way there individually. Of course, this strange profusion of late visitors heading singly in the direction of the great tower was itself suspicious to the alert guards, however reasonable it might have been had rumours not been flying, and therefore each conspirator was intercepted before he arrived. This was usually done quietly enough. They were then flung hilariously and triumphantly into prison.

Peace seemed to reign for a few hours. Unfortunately though, there was another tower which itself was not very far from the centre of the city, and a goodly proportion of the conspirators, presumably including the less intelligent ones, had fetched up here in individual arrivals, although some had just followed the others, supposing it to be the place from which the attack must be due to be launched. It was not so central a location, and it was directly reachable by a far greater number of routes than was the great tower which they were supposed to have been assembling at. Indeed, in some ways, although certainly not in all, it was a choice preferable to the site actually selected, given that circumstances were as they happened to be. We may think of ourselves as being in Copenhagen, if we absolutely must. This group waited for a few hours, increasingly surprised at how few of them had decided to turn up. They then had to make a choice as to whether to return home, or whether to proceed with the insurrection even though their numbers were so few. Stirred by the thought that the others had abandoned them, as if they were not worthy of their trust, they decided to try to justify themselves, to see things through, not a few of them suspecting that somehow or other they might still fall in with their colleagues up ahead.

Normally, of course, they would have had no chance of success. However, since the defending guards believed – with good reason – that they had just foiled the uprising which lively rumour had had it was going to be set in motion at around this time, the defending forces were by now widely dispersed, largely inattentive, and to a considerable extent incapacitated through a celebratory excess of alcohol. Thus the offensive met with virtually none of the stern opposition which it would otherwise have faced at numerous points all the way along its extended route. In short, the attack succeeded and the old rulers were comprehensively driven out. Those who had assembled at the correct great tower, who had been imprisoned earlier, were now released. As they contained all the more promising leading figures, they soon took over the burden of command.

A little later, the central tower was demolished, and all traces of it were expunged from the written records. Then, not long after that, the more remote tower was dismantled stone by stone, and was quietly moved to the site which the great central tower had previously occupied, where it was carefully rebuilt. This was known as the Restoration. Then the bodies of the group of those conspirators of the unsuccessful first batch who had been killed while trying to escape or avoid arrest were buried on what had previously been the site of the more remote tower. Then a few reports of brave battles and ugly skirmishes were invented over the years by a gifted set of literary placemen to account for these deaths, which it was otherwise distinctly difficult to explain away. And thus was reality brought into line with the known facts.

Great meetings are now held there every year to celebrate these events, and there are always many passionate speeches made and numerous exciting parades. The people are exhorted to be proud of their heritage and never to forget their magnificent past. Most of them are thrilled and patriotic anyway, and scarcely need such a reminder.

Incident in Upshot Creek

Wearily, Jake clambered onto the bed in his little hotel room. What a grim day it had been! Yep. Mighty grim. He was too tired to take off his boots, or even to wash himself, though he much liked an occasional wash. All that gross unpleasantness with the Macavitty Gang had taken a great deal out of him. At least his window would give him a good view over the main street of the town, he thought, if you could properly call Upshot Creek a town, in case anything else should happen between now and sun-up.

He was sure it had been a mistake to accept the nomination as sheriff. The trouble was he had been in a state of altered consciousness when the position was offered to him and it all happened before he had had time to think about how unwise it was. And even if he had had time to reflect, what then? Someone had to do it. All the butchery and banditry and brigandage around these parts, the terrorising of innocent citizens, not to mention some of the guilty ones, had gone on for long enough. For far too long. What was he supposed to do? Run away from his responsibilities forever? Refuse to shoulder the burden which his society, even if it was a society that hadn't been all that good to him in the past, had nonetheless legitimately asked him to bear? None of the voices in Jake's ears would have let him do that without raising a strong protest. Yessir, a mighty protest.

And now the varmints had gone and burned down his fine new house, even though his pet dog, Confucius, had still been inside it. Well, he could survive that. Confucius couldn't, of course, but he, Jake, could. They would pay for it. They would pay only what they owed, but that would be enough to be getting on with. Until that was done, he would carry about forever in a small purse round his neck as a grim reminder of his duty one of Confucius's detached ears, still incredibly neat and pretty. He put his guns on the table directly at his side, lay his greasy head back on the even greasier pillow, and almost instantly fell asleep.

About an hour or so later he was woken up by saucy hands pawing all over him. However, it turned out it was only Moll from downstairs, along with a couple of her friends, Riot and Conchita. Angrily, he got up and bundled them out of the door. He was not going to have any of that nonsense happening while he was in charge of this precarious polity. No, sirree. A timely reminder always to check that the doors were safely locked. He turned the key in the lock and went back to his bed. They had a strange sense of humour, some of the people in these parts. Let them spread ugly rumours about him if they wanted to. He had more important things to worry about. All right, they had buried his beloved Evelyn in a mud plot west of the Coblewhonies near on five years ago now; but that still didn't mean it was right to be unfaithful to the memory. No, sirree. I'll need to stop thinking 'No, sirree' to myself, he thought, as he drifted back into the welcoming arms of Morpheus, that well-known nimble Greek fairy.

Soon he was deep in a troubled and complex dream in which he and an angel who called himself Looni were trying to play Schubert duets on a piano. Looni was trying to give him a message from beyond, to the effect that the secret of the universe was written in the scrap of paper that he was sure he had seen stuffed down the front of Moll's low-cut and sensational if cheap dress. Jake was arguing that this was impossible, as the woman was illiterate in all her various languages, of which there were possibly only one. Anyway, he didn't want to look for it. He just didn't, that was all. What was he meant to be telling her anyway, while he was looking for the message? She would probably leap to the conclusion that he was in some way sexually interested in her. Looni laughed long and loud at this; and then sneered that, as Jake was a man, he naturally could not be expected to understand very much about all this, since he was completely incapable of bearing children.

Jake instinctively felt that this was a low blow, really unfair, since the angel was male too, and he told him as much in forthright, manly terms. At which tears started to the angel's lovely big eyes, and he said that that was quite wrong. He was actually a she, as would be quite obvious if he, Jake, had bothered to take even the most cursory look. What cowards men could be, even here in Upshot Creek, where some had formerly been renowned for their almost incredible bravery! Jake apologised profusely at once, although at heart he was not convinced. Looni could see this intuitively of course. She started to try to lift up her dazzling lacey white shift, using arms and wings, in order to demonstrate the considerable extent of his mistake in the most direct and irrefutable way. Jake, horrified at what he might see, whatever it was, sought to prevent her by manual force. And all the while the two of

135

them were continuing to do their level best to play the F minor fantasia of the immortal Franz P. Schubert – a beautiful but challenging piece, which it can be difficult enough to get right even under less trying circumstances.

The terrible thought struck him that to some extent – he tried desperately to see clearly but it was as if he couldn't get his neck round far enough – he must surely be playing at least some of the notes with his toes and perhaps even with his penis. If so, this was, obviously, dreadful. What if the angel noticed? Was she playing with her wings? How would she react? Clearly a public recital was now thoroughly out of the question – unless he was able to change his technique wholesale in the bare hour or so that remained (as far as he could remember) before the recital was due to be given. And how many people were ever able to do that? It was an unfair and unrealistic demand to make of him, no mistake about that. What? Only an hour? And had it even been advertised properly?

Whatever might be going on, the music that resulted was an oddly compelling cacophony of shrieks, protestations, wrong notes, and strange rhythmic hammerings from somewhere or other. A small man with intense eyes suddenly appeared beside them, and tried to drag them apart, crying out, 'How can you quarrel, my herring, when you have just created the music of the future together?' At which Looni burst into tears, reached down below the piano, evidently with one of her well-worth-looking-after feet, and brought up a tiny baby which she deposited, with a certain lack of considerateness, slap-bang right down in the music-holder. 'Argue with that!' she cried, convulsively, before disappearing upwards and outwards. Jake was wrestling with the problem of how best to frame his apology to someone right beside him, given that he was not quite sure what the apology was for, or who was right beside him, though it might well be the impressario, when he shuddered and woke up.

It was dark by now, and strangely silent. A cold air was drifting silently in from the Rio Celeste. He turned off the lamp, which had evidently begun to run out of fuel not long before. It was clear to him at once that he would not be sleeping again for a long while. Slowly he got out of bed and crossed to the window. There was moonlight on the street outside. Nothing looked to be happening there. One or two of the curtained windows along the opposite side still showed lights at them, but it all was quiet. There was some sort of call not far away. A creaking door, or a horse moving, or perhaps a thief. Or perhaps all three. It looked as if nothing serious would be happening for quite a while.

He found another lamp on the table by the window. It still had some fuel in it. He lit it, then went over to the bags he had brought into the room with him. He opened the smallest of them and took out from it some tobacco, some whisky, a dog's leash, and three or four books he had brought with him. From these he selected Cicero's *De Natura Deorum*, and he went over to the window, to leaf through it there. It certainly contained some good stuff, that much was clear. But was it quite right for the time and place? What else was there? Berlioz's autobiography he had nearly finished. He was rationing himself to a little per day now. It wouldn't do to have exhausted his quota before even the sun had risen. And he didn't feel much in the mood just at the moment for either that crazyhead Pushkin or for Sir William Hamilton, the last of whom seemed at times to cherish some extremely peculiar ideas regarding cognition, to say the least.

Still, what else was there to do? You did the best you could. What else could you do? He would have liked to

137

practise the artistic, aesthetic flower-arranging which a family friend from the east had once taught him in the peace and quiet of the night back in New England, but there just weren't any of the right flowers available at present. And, obviously, there would be no point in waking anyone up in Upshot Creek just to ask for them. It would probably end up doing more harm than good. So he stood mutely by the window and continued to ponder.

Which, if it is true, is extremely strange. And I'll tell you exactly why. I had always understood that the man couldn't read. Take it from me. Why should I lie to you of all people? And if that's true – which it is – then I suppose he must still be asleep. At the very least. Certainly I didn't hear a shot. And I certainly didn't fire one myself. Strange. It's incredibly quiet too for such a rough town, isn't it? Why are you here in the room as well, by the way? I think maybe, if you value your own safety, you had better leave. Don't worry. I'll spin a yarn to cover your retreat. Quick! Here he comes! No. Wait a moment. I think it's maybe only a false alarm. Still: better go. Better safe than sorry.

The Mistake

It was dark and foggy and he wasn't really looking where he was going. Also he had gone this way on hundreds of afternoons before so there was really no particular need to look about at all for much of the time. Or so it seemed to him anyway. Where these cigarettes kept disappearing to was more of a mystery. Much more of a mystery. He couldn't be smoking them all, he knew that much. Could he? Yet they kept on going missing. Day after day. Perhaps the air itself was smoking them. That would explain it. In a sense.

Anyway at least there weren't many people about in this weather at this time of day. He turned briskly into the shop doorway, glad of the shelter, then opened the door and went through. Not wishing to seem too enthusiastic, he didn't look up for a second or two. When he did, a distinctly bizarre sight greeted his eyes. A couple of naked menlike figures, whisking tails, were engaged in smoothing down the sides of a small rowing-boat-like vehicle in the middle of a bright but dimly lit room which seemed to have a very thick tree growing in the middle of it. He stopped, startled. What was this? They looked up at him as he entered with neither great enthusiasm nor particular surprise. They were evidently quite unimpressed. Rather than wait to explain his error, he apologised in something of a confused mumble and left at once. As far as he could tell, they at once went nonchalantly back to work. He was not even sure that they had heard him.

So what? A few yards up ahead he turned into another doorway, a very similar one, and this time, to his relief, he found that he was indeed inside the shop he had been seeking. He laconically purchased a packet of cigarettes, a newspaper which was being offered at a reduced price that day, a large bar of chocolate, a magazine full of pictures of half-naked women and girls pretending to be laboratory scientists, and a couple of thin-pointed pens which had black ink in them. He was particularly glad to have remembered to buy the pens. He had been meaning to buy more of them for days, but hitherto he had always forgotten about it until he was back up the stairs in his home. This, obviously, could be pretty maddening.

He lit a cigarette on his return journey. It reassured him and helped to pass the time. It was still very foggy. You wondered where it all came from sometimes. No-one seemed to have anticipated it. It had evidently just happened. Dropped out of nowhere. An occasional car might pass by very near, but he wouldn't be able to see more of it than a smear of light flooding out of a darker patch that accompanied it. It was all most peculiar. Not that he was particularly interested to know who it was who was passing him down this street. It would be no-one he knew, doubtless. After all, it usually was.

When he got home he began by making sure that all the doors were safely and carefully closed. What was coming next was the bit that he always enjoyed most.

It was important not to rush. It was important to savour it. This he, as usual, tried his best to do. All things considered, he would say that so far it all had gone rather well. But that could still change. Things could always at any point change considerably.

A Problem in Engineering

At the end of another long day's work, he climbs slowly up the hill. The bad moments have come again. Still, so far they have invariably proved transitory. When first he bought a house up here, beyond even where the municipal roadways reached, his mother had told him on her first visit (which she achieved with considerable difficulty, claiming that it was shortening her life) that if he stayed here long enough he would eventually find himself struggling to make it back home here at nights. It would just be too much of an effort. He hadn't doubted that, somehow, it was true; as if in some other universe than this; but he had laughed anyway, and he had been vaguely annoyed when she used this trivial difficulty as an apparently valid excuse for visiting him so rarely. It hadn't occurred to him that something that was only a question of physical effort could constitute a serious excuse for not doing something so central to a life as visiting one of your own children – particularly when he, unlike some others he could name, had not left the city. True, she had died only three years later; there was that too.

Of course, there were several of his own children

143

whom he himself did not visit now, but that was different. For that he had legitimate excuses, many of them matters of principle. One lived in South America, for one thing. She had been there for five years; even though he in his whole life had never so much as spent five seconds on that continent, or even seen its coastline from afar. Neither, as best he could remember, had either of his own parents done so. And of their parents? What of them? For all he knew of any of them, they could have passed one year in every country south of Panama. They could have been twice his height. They could have been beheaded for murder, or drowned at sea, for all he knew. But he had produced her, and she was now over there. Is this why you produced other people? So they could go to South America? It didn't seem an entirely convincing process somehow.

As for the others, they were hardly worth thinking about. He would not be forced to retire, surely? He was too valuable. The younger ones might have a surer grasp of the newer techniques; but none of them had remotely the depth of insight into the principles and history of the good old profession as he himself had, surely? Surely the core of it would never change. Surely it would at least have the goodness to last out until he had retired. After that it could do what it liked. What did it matter. It would be such a relief to get back home, and at last be able to put his feet up and relax. True, his wife was no longer there; but what had they had to say to each other for the last quarter of a century? Oh, a weighty number of words, no doubt; but it seemed to him he could just as well have said virtually all of them to another person entirely.

A little further up the slope, and then there would be the gap in the fencing which contained the overhung lane he was to follow. It was always such a relief to him when he turned into that lane. It meant he could now afford to stop worrying as to what might happen to him if he were to miss his footing on the steeper part of the climb. He no longer had to worry that he might, for instance, fall, entirely lose purchase on the ground, and begin to roll back down the hill, gathering momentum all the time as he descended; ripping destructively on straight through one or two gardens; perhaps going right through an open front door and smashing out through a flimsy back one, probably harshly interrupting a quiet domestic scene; rocketing through the graveyard, hopefully not during a service; then racing through the distinguished inner suburb at an ever-increasing speed; hurtling next past the administrative centre, the railway station, the cathedral and possibly the finest new hospital in the country, certainly in that part of the country; before at length reaching the quay, launching magnificently into the air in a graceful high arc, and falling with an immense splash of shocked water some considerable part of the way over towards the nearest offshore island, for good measure disrupting the rare wildlife in a possibly quite serious and long-lasting way. Not that, oh Lord, whatever else might be in store for me!

Whenever he turned off into the lane, he knew that all that could be safely ruled out for another day at least. All he had to worry about now was either having an aneurism, or else being fired at from behind one of the many windows which were hidden everywhere in the foliage around him; or maybe finding that his home had at long last been taken away while his back was turned. That was still a recurring nightmare. Nor did he wish to discover that the doors were all unlocked, even though there was no-one in the house just at the moment.

No. His wife had been entirely wrong. It was a rough

145

old world, and one had to be as careful as one could be. Ah yes; there was the house. Still there. Good. That at least is not in South America. Some things remain stable, even in this ungrateful life.

As he approached it he began to worry that perhaps he had really moved away to another flat on a lower level only fairly recently, and that really he no longer ought to be coming up here at all. Could that be true? Would one really forget something like that? If not, why did that picture come to mind just then? Mere coincidence? He brought all his keys out of his pocket and looked at them. Hello. Three sets of keys! Not without significance, surely? No; no. How could it possibly be? Three sets of keys! And a lot of people didn't have any at all! Brilliant!

Or Valparaiso

What now? Walking round the corner more slowly than ever today, this morning, as far as I can estimate it, right into the sudden cold wind now we are clear of the wall, but it has never stopped me yet. It won't stop me today. It won't. Not without a fight. Though I would rather it fought somebody else. Away and fight somebody else. Go on. Those tranters that drive their bikes anywhere for instance, and cause accidents. Myself, I can't remember the last time I went out looking for trouble. Apart from anything else, it finds you anyway. So why encourage it? Just stroke its back if it'll let you, and tell it to get lost. Or ask it to, if you would rather be polite; but I think telling it is probably the best bet. Or break its neck; it would be ideal if you could do that. Break its neck. That would certainly put a stop to it. With a bit of luck.

Oh well. Still going. What now? I think now would be rather a good moment for me to transfer some membraneous material from my troubled interior onto the in some ways even more troubled pavement. Yeurggh. Good. A notable success. Now what? Five years ago now since she went, and her stuff is still cluttering up

147

the drawers and sideboard, and nothing is worth moving. Well, I am moving myself, true, if you could call it moving, particularly when you consider what I used to do; but I am moving myself mainly to get some milk, or so I thought when I finally managed to find the key and leave, since the stuff I got last week has already gone off. The interior of cows, and so forth. An odd business indeed.

I would say everything goes off. I am tired. It is a tiring job being so indomitable. Do I have to be quite such a good example to others? Does it really do them any good? Does it interest them at all? Still, you have to be brave I suppose; because if you aren't brave, then a lot of people from various concerned departments might just take it into their finely educated minds to come and seek you out and descend on you one fine day just when you think things are going better than usual, and cart you away without so much as by-your-leave to somewhere that no-one gets out of. They probably wouldn't even want to let you know the address. Particularly if they get wind of the fact that you are living there on your own. Like what happened to that old fool downstairs that we have never seen since, who used to play German marching-songs from the last war late at night over and over and over again. Perhaps he has finally been able to join up. Perhaps he has finally got to lead the invasion. He had an Italian name. Or more likely someone finally managed to get a complaint listened to after years of trying. All the same, I wish I had kept my own gun. That would at least give you more possibilities. If the worst came to the worst. Or even if it didn't.

I don't know. Maybe I should have spent more time up on the roof of the old building in all those years when I still had the chance. But at least I am still able to get out of the house. I am not drunk and incapable, like some neighbours I could mention who can hardly be half my age. I can still aim a good kick at the local dogs, if need be, and often it is. Get out of it! I can still cross the road, even if cars always appear right out of nowhere just as I start, often maroon or red ones for some reason; I can still buy a newspaper; I could still bet on the horses if I wanted to. As it happens, I don't want to. I have made my choice here. They don't seem to have as much life in them as they used to have. I prefer just to watch them on the television, though I wish they would spend more time actually running their races rather than just walking about and being talked about by over-educated ponces who must be making a very nice living for doing next to nothing, for something I could do as well myself, or anyone else for that matter. But we were never given the chance, were we? We had to do something real instead.

I just wonder when it's going to happen, that's all. I must be quite a bit older by now than that uncle of mine who dropped dead in the street longer ago than I can get to calculate. Fifty-seven years ago. Fifty-six or fifty-seven. Can't be fifty-eight yet, can it? Whatever it was, I met him only once. Nearly sixty. He had been to Valparaiso. Or the ship was called the *Valparaiso*. Or maybe both. I've seen it on the map. I went home and checked it up. Years ago. It's the capital of Aconagua Province – I can still remember that – in Chile, which is a very funny shape for a real country. I seem to recall that an archbishop lives there. At least an archbishop. They'll have changed him by now no doubt; at least once. And this is still such a terrible crossing. All that mess on the streets. And the cans. I think we should all eat more dogs and rabbits. I could build a ship with all the cans I have kicked out of my way in my time. Yes. Yes. I think I have managed to be a convincing member of the working class. I certainly hope so.

However, here's the right close for it. I think this close should be just right for it. Yes indeed. There's nobody that's going to stop me now. Just let them try it. Ten minutes should do it, and then I'll re-emerge at a run, a magnificent run; moving with such acceleration and elegance that heads will turn to watch me as I hurry down the main road past them, even though they pretend not to be impressed. I am beyond caring about their impressions. There's not much I need to change. The clothing, of course; but not much more than that. An older world awaits me, I have always firmly believed that. Or perhaps I ought to call it a younger world. A different sort of world anyway. A world of speed, among other things.

A Sample of the Ancient Wisdom

A stinging, freezing rain whipped against the inadequately protected little croft on the exposed slope where it faced the sea on the small and remote island of Snorka. Rangvald staggered back up the muddy, jagged path, on the last lap of his return home from the distant village where he had been working on the collapsed communal outdoor latrine, which had had to be repaired as quickly as possible in the cold weather of spring. How he was looking forward to the comparative warmth of the interior, and his beautiful if ageing wife, Revevag, whose interior (he knew) could very often in some uncanny way be even warmer – oh, curse his failing powers! And there would be broth too, and the distant cry of oppressed birds, and possibly even the radio would be working again and it would broadcast a story such as he loved, with snow in it, and the sea, and a humane cry against the encroachments, powerful and financially well founded but surely not irresistible, of an increasingly technological and soulless civilisation, which could offer him nothing, except perhaps for a few thousand minor domestic and everyday improvements. But what of the soul, eh? What of his soul?

What did they think of that? Why did they never address themselves to that problem?

'A fine day it is, and a brave, brisk one, Master Rangvald!' called out Norrie with naive, religious wonder from the depths of the ditch as he passed him.

'I'm sorry, Norrie,' he replied with a strange exaltation. 'Almost failed I to see thee there. Aye, indeed. Ferkleegen it be. The stu'ibs ha' quig'ged throug' t'e absent sun, an' t'e freggens ha'e b'rgled mo' or le' indiscriminately o' the hafdom!' he replied, with a cheerfulness which he was in fact far from feeling. Though facts themselves are things also without feeling often enough, I should say. Then on he went and through the slightly rotting door, which he knew he must soon fix before it collapsed colossally inwards, perhaps killing an infant, if one were to be playing beside it. One never had so far. There was at least that to be grateful for to the good Lord, wherever he was.

His wife was sitting by the window, a strange, eerie light playing about her hair. 'I finished peeling the vegetables long ago, Rangvald Thungg,' she said, with that curious formality of diction which was one of the things that had first won his heart. It was that and her young biceps which had most done it, perhaps. Who can say for sure? The heart of another is a strange beast, which wanders at night weeping through territory which it does not seek formal and written permission to enter. How could it, when it knows neither how to write nor how to read? Truly does the good book say much the same as that. That is well enough known on the island of Snorka, and elsewhere too, if the truth be told. Yea, even on the mainland they know that. So he thought to himself, for he enjoyed a grim joke. As had his forefathers. It was part of the uralt traditions of the place.

Then he sat himself down on the broken seat, for she already had possession of the seat which had integrity. Her face reflected from the cracked mirror behind her, and he was struck yet again by a consideration of her beauty. He opened his mouth to tell her so, but she forestalled him by her powerful complaint. And she said to him: It is many years now, Rangvald, since last you told me that my penis was beautiful. Many years, by the dark heart of Saint Parvus. Thirteen, I think. Perhaps five and a half. A magical number indeed. Can your so-called modern science tell you anything about that? Although there was a time when you used to waken me up in the middle of the night to mention the fact to me in conversation until I had to beg you not to. For you were also waking the sheep. You have forgotten that I suppose, Rangvald. And for this omission the time has come when you must die. For I must now go back to the realm I came from, and I must take all the air in this wet cottage with me, and you must expire for lack of respiration. That sad moment may no longer be postponed. I shall think of you always when my thoughts return to this cold world, from the warm world of the silken light.

And Rangvald, who was sure he had told his wife how beautiful her penis was certainly last year, and quite possibly at the beginning of this year too, was shocked by her behaviour. And he walked out of the house and did not return until the same time the following week. Or perhaps it was even longer. For not only was he terrified out of his wits, but he had been drinking all that time, sombre potations to God for his mercy and variousness; thanks to a fortunate shipwreck just offshore which he had been the sole observer of – for, though he was sadly unable (thanks to the inscrutable, or perhaps I should say, unkennable, agency of Providence) to save any of the poor, God-intoxicated Christian souls who were caught in that foundering and were lost, he had at least managed to save a great deal of the hard liquor which had been aboard. And yet, when eventually he returned home, hoping it might be safe, to his astonishment he found that his wife, Revevag, was sitting in the other chair this time, still there in the house, entirely wrapped in enveloping outdoor clothing; and when he entered, she leapt up eagerly to greet him, like the young girl she had formerly been and which many young girls still were, crying out: 'Daddy Bear! Forgive me for my earlier misjudgement of thee!'

At which point there was a knock at the door, and the sound of several voices outside, although he had observed no-one there or near there as he had come running up the pathway as fast as he could. And at that point Revevag (it's a Lapp name), with love in her eyes, divested herself of her attire in the twinkling of an instant, far more quickly than he would ever have supposed was possible; and she seemed to gleam like the purest light and have any age which he required. Sunlight on the still water was nothing to her or the shimmer she purveyed. And she asked him: Rangvald, oh most provocative of men. What has this taught you? Tell me the right answer and all our troubles are past. What has this taught you?

And Rangvald replied: Yes, I shall tell thee what it has taught me. To whom if not to you? It has taught me, my beloved woman, that if Death were a person, he would be the greatest bore imaginable. What a dreary old windbag. And Revevag broke into a wondrous smile and replied: We must go somewhere at once, my enchanted Rangvald. And do something. Or perhaps various things. For how can we do nothing? And he responded: Right. Okay. Sure thing. Lead on. I am beyond fear now. My life has

154

disappeared down a certain unique set of holes and is, I dare say, now all the better for it. And the rain continued to hammer against the windows. As indeed did a person outside the house, who thought he had come to dispossess them.

Quite a few Biographies

It is not easy to be accurate at such a distance in time, but I shall try my best. Very well. It was extremely late in the evening before I managed to shake myself free of all the manifold duties of the day. I returned quickly to my hotel room, where I prepared myself as speedily as I could in all the richest treasures of the finery I had brought there with me. A great and much longed-for opportunity had at last arisen. I was quite determined to make the greatest impression that I possibly could. This, I determined, was going to be a night to remember, whatever else there may have been to sully my stay, and to render it, in business terms, something of a disappointment. This would make up for everything.

Very soon, everything was as I would have wished it to be. All was right. Any further preparations would have been just as likely to dampen the effect I was seeking to make as to enhance it. I dare say some improvements were still possible – after all, some improvements always are, no matter what it is, since nothing is perfect – but it was a question of needing to make lengthy and laborious efforts to produce tiny degrees of betterment, and I knew instinctively that this would be more trouble than it was worth. After all, I am no scientist. For one thing, I lack the absolutely necessary commitment to truth.

Thrilled with the anticipation of what was surely to follow, I gave my appearance a final check in the mirror, saw nothing there to give me pause, and lingered for a moment in open-hearted admiration before hurrying out of the room, intent on reaching as soon as possible the legendary pleasure quarter nearby – the scene of song, ecstasy, romance, laughter and no doubt innumerable other things besides, nearly all of them admirable; and a location already, I felt, familiar to me from so many books and shows and films and dreams and magazines and God knows what.

Only five minutes later, I dismissed the taxi and its obviously perverted and cretinous driver, and I strode eagerly and confidently through the little archway which led to the main square. All was still right. It was a magnificent scene of lights and gardens and open windows. I thought I could even hear music play. I am almost sure I did. I did. I know I did. However, most unfortunately, there was absolutely no-one there. No-one. Nor, indeed, were there any striking signs to indicate that people had been there recently. The place was, to be brief, entirely deserted and quiet.

I was, I admit, flummoxed. Bamboozled. Taken aback. I had no idea how to proceed. In the end, I did no more than wander slowly through the square for perhaps the best part of an hour, and then, when I had reached the other end, I made my mind up on an impulse and walked swiftly back to the hotel, where I at once went to bed, and had a damn good night's sleep. That would be something, at least.

I awoke feeling refreshed and revivified. Any tears had long since dried. I felt I was ready for anything. The excitement of the previous day still ran riot through my veins. Moving softly and silently, so as not to awaken the adorable, unknown figure who was lying asleep in the wildly disordered sheets beside me, I clambered stealthily out of bed, made my way to the bathroom, fell heavily onto my side and, in the confusion of my immense joy, I perhaps swallowed a few dozen potentially lethal pills. I then sat down on the sombre-hued bidet and, with a sense of the appropriateness of absolutely everything, I waited patiently for the end. I must have fallen asleep next, I suppose.

When I woke up, I found I was looking after a hospital for authentically distressed indigenes somewhere in the Andes. Oh well. It is tiring work, certainly; but it is also so unspeakably rewarding. Unspeakably. At times their gratitude moves me to tears; but I have so far managed to avoid hitting out at anyone. Don't judge me. You should hear how they talk. It looks quite possible that I shall in fact live out the last of my days here, right to the bitter end. Jesus Christ, will no-one come here to save me? But, no; no. They would so much rather save everyone else. The immensely broad river is very beautiful, flowing away silently in the late evening as it does; and then again flowing away in the morning. And at noon too. The speed varies occasionally. Help! Help! Please help.

Social Beasts

A few remarks about life would not come amiss now, I think, said a man with whom I struck up a combative and ultimately unsuccessful acquaintance while I was visiting that open-air market which they have every Friday in the large canyon at the foot of Buccleuch Street. Locals will know instantly what I am talking about. We discovered we were old school acquaintances. He appeared not to recognise me, but I was quite certain of many previous sightings of him: including one in which he screamed when another youth, much taller, with timing which was impressive enough in its way, unexpectedly caught hold of his genitals through the legs from behind. (It was an all-boys' school, after all, and it was in large part run by a religious brotherhood.) And another characteristic vignette comes to mind, of when, attempting a Latin translation in which, although intelligent, he took no interest and could see no point, in response to a master who was forever telling us to think of the English (which was often derived directly from the Latin) he rendered *prodere* (meaning, in this instance, 'to betray') as 'to prod'; clearly relishing the hopelessness of it all as he did so and probably also baiting the master as a sort of vengeful bonus. What a lad, eh?

Such of his red hair as was not now greying had by and large disappeared by this date, as had my recollection of his name, which he did nothing to refresh. The re-encounter, however, was entirely fortuitous. Certainly it was on my part, although, of course, for all I know he may have been secretly following me for years, in an anguished and ultimately not very successful attempt to re-establish contact. We all know that such things must happen often enough. Why should we always fly from the obvious explanations?

As it happens, we were both mightily interested in acquiring a large stuffed and mounted example of a shark which stood out remarkably, as it would, among a heap of rubbish which some little old lady (who was originally from, as she insisted, a tiny village called Society) had somehow managed to acquire – no doubt not entirely legally. I cannot really explain the attraction which such beasts have for me. I suppose I just feel there is something wonderfully and convincingly Old Testament about their appearance and attitudes. Anyway, I took it for granted that this one was a Common Spiny Dogfish – *Squalus Acanthias* – which can live in vast shoals and is fairly common in the North Sea, which is not too far away, all things considered, from Buccleuch Street, which is where my grandmother used to stay when first I became aware of her existence. The house is still there. Not so, alas, my grandmother. Certainly she cannot have been the woman who was selling the shark, for she is dead. As indeed was the shark. Something they have in common there, though they belong to quite different living kingdoms.

Whatshisname, however – was it Queen? something like that – was contemptuously dismissive of my opinion.

As he pointed out, harried by teachers whom he simply did not get on with, he had left school at an earlier age than he ought to have done in order to work in the local fishmarket (now, eheu, no longer there) and he was absolutely certain that this fellow was one of the Smooth Dogfishes, the *Triakidae* – specifically *Mustelus mustelus* (which personally I think is a rather stupid name for a shark) – which is widely found along the European coasts. If it's a squalus, he asked challengingly – like you say it is – then where are the sharp poisonous spines in front of the dorsal fins? This was an objection which, to my regret, I found a curious and profound difficulty in parrying.

In view of this development, I thought it more appropriate for him to have the stuffed shark than for me to do so. He, evidently elated, relaxed sufficiently to drop his guard and, as he thought, sought to reward me with a few observations about what life had taught him. I was not particularly interested in them, needless to say – not at all, in fact – but I thought that here would at least be a useful opportunity for me to test out the powers of a new battery-operated dictaphone which I had acquired five minutes before, at another stall, in part exchange for some silver knives and forks of a certain value that I had wanted to get rid of rather quickly. Consequently I recorded his next remarks, such as they were.

Do doo doo do doo patang. Of course (he began), to be killed by one of these great shaggy or razor-toothed animals of land or sea is in itself bad enough, not something many people would be eager to have a piece of, is it? – but it is surely the fact that sharks see us as *food* when they attack us that makes the prospect of such an encounter so especially disagreeable to people. Yummy! They are not motivated by some abstract enmity – a word which, until I was over forty, I truly thought was pronounced and written 'emnity' – or by any intuitive desire to clear space of threats. No. Not primarily that. Evidently, for some inadequate reason best known to themselves, they have categorised us as essentially physical objects. Eh? As something we might point to in a restaurant. Us with our thoughts wandering through eternity, eh (Milton), and our belief that the universe has personal feelings for us, and so forth. What a carry-on! Sharks, in short, are rather a challenge to the religious and spiritual intuitions of many of us – to their sense that it cannot be right to see us as physical entities, as things you eat for God's sake, like sardines or oysters or loaves of bread or fish suppers or my wife's leftovers. I take it this thing is working, is it? Shouldn't there be a light somewhere? What?

Oh. Right. I hadn't noticed. Okay. Right. Ah yes. I know what it was. How we can eat, in restaurant after restaurant, all sorts of things from the sea. Think of it. There are more of them than there are of us, are there not? In private house after private house too, of course, I'm not trying to deny that. One kitchen after another. Or the best room. Stuff which we don't even know the proper name for. Perhaps one in a million does. You don't, obviously.

Oysters, for instance. They have been that way for a tediously large number of millions of years. I cut the right number out of a paper once but I lost it. When we don't even know how it is they must live; whether they dream or not; what sort of life is possible for them – how the moving bits move, if any; how they propel themselves through the water, if they do; how they can live without moving from the seabed, if they do; how they see or feel, if they do; how they think, if they do – presumably they don't. What would they think about? Not water, that is for sure.

Listen. How is it that some people can spend an entire

life searching for them and can have spent decades scooping up these things which live for perhaps a few days only – I don't actually know enough about them myself – and can find them in thousands after thousands of places, perhaps in schools in fact, and not know all that much about them. In fact, they might not even know what they taste like. Or perhaps only for the taste. The taste. People eat them in a wide range of exclusive restaurants too, knowing nothing else. They might as well be stones. Maybe they are, of a sort. Eh? Think of it. Friends get drowned; or bones slowly turn rotting and ruined; hands get gnarled and swollen and painful for the rest of their life. For what? To know what? To make a living? Soon the great sea covers all. Eh? You know what I mean? As they used to say in school. The cruel, grey, in some senses deeply homosexual ocean. No; no. Just a little joke. But it's certainly provocative, isn't it? Yes. Don't you go this way? Oh, all right. Here you are then. Might catch you again later, eh? Bye. Myself, this is another of those days I'll never forget. Of course, you can never be quite sure about things like that. Still; I don't think I will. Do you?

Some More Eternal Delight

At the start, all went as smoothly as anyone could have wished. Indeed, even when it began to go wrong – if that is what it did – it did so in a wonderfully seamless manner. I suppose it is hard to say when anyone started to feel the first undeniable tremors of uncertainty. One might have thought that these would surely have come from one of the musicians, and that is still very likely to be the case. However, as things are at the moment, it would, I am sure, be tactless and unnecessary to intervene merely on the plea of an attempt at a deeper understanding of whatever it was that was going on. The phenomenon, I am assured, is a complex one – which I do not doubt – and it is still under active investigation. Or so I have heard. For myself, I have been much too busy lately to have had time to make involved personal enquiries. For all I know, the phenomenon has already been fully explained elsewhere.

That the manuscript of a lost fantasy for piano and violin by Franz Peter Schubert should have been discovered in Glasgow of all places was odd enough in itself. That it should be first performed there at the City Hall by an internationally famous pair of artists – well, perhaps that could hardly as such be quibbled with. However, the fact that it was due to be given a first performance there before any published edition had been put out, and therefore before any authorised recording of the new work could be made, was greeted in some quarters with a quizzical and elegantly raised eyebrow. Dark rumours had begun to percolate in not particularly well-informed media circles about gorgeously vague 'production difficulties' – and those who had always been sceptical about the authenticity of the recently discovered manuscript were succoured in their disbelief by the numerous small signs of stress and strain which were freely discernible here and there. As if any proceedings so fraught with potential significance could reasonably be expected to be entirely devoid of stresses and strains!

That the manuscript had been discovered, to be somewhat more specific, stuffed inside the drone of a set of discarded bagpipes found lying in a gutter at the southeast junction of Elderslie Street and Berkeley Street, had of course at first led in numerous places to the automatic and (I suppose) easily understandable assumption that the work could not possibly be genuine. How on earth could it ever have got there, unrecorded and unchanced upon through so many silent years? Nonetheless, after a very few months had passed and some beautifully weighted and promulgated initial analyses and investigations had been made, only a few diehards were still holding out for fraud as their breathing became more and more difficult. The general capitulation had been particularly sped by a gifted trio of Viennese scholars who had been brought in by a profoundly unconvinced civil servant with an axe of his own to grind; and who, to everyone's astonishment including their own, had very quickly been forced to the conclusion that it was indeed a genuine work – a conclusion profoundly unwelcome to them, but one which their scholarly devotion to the truth simply did not permit them to continue to resist in the face of such a powerful battery of developing evidence. We salute them here, and once again take the opportunity to applaud such a magnificent example of intellectual honesty. There is a lesson here for all of us, surely.

Once the broad consensus of approval had been reached, events tending to consolidate it followed thick and fast. So signal an opportunity to drive home the status of Glasgow as possibly the world's single greatest centre of artistic excellence – with the possible exception of Aarhus – could hardly be passed up. Two of the foremost virtuosi whom mere cash could entice to reschedule their previously solidly arranged commitments were engaged to perform the piece at a special matinée concert, the whole thing to be finished with a splendid civic reception for all concerned, to be combined with a full-scale press conference in the Function Suite upstairs.

Thus it was that at one o'clock sharp on the afternoon of the long-awaited day, the gifted duo walked out onto the stage in front of the proud and delighted audience. After a tantalising pause for tuning – during which the solemn realisation of just how momentous and epoch-making an event this represented was perhaps fully appreciated by many for the first time – the opening bars, released from their many decades of cruel silence, soared over the assembled heads, and then sped out into an auditorium which drank up the music as greedily as the parched earth welcomes the rain – but without the sense of desperation which such an image may possibly conjure up. For several minutes, the enchantment continued at its peak. Ah, how wonderful those minutes were!

Of course, a fantasia is, by its nature, usually less rigidly

structured than a suite is or a sonata, and it was some time
– perhaps a quarter of an hour or so – before the first signs
of restlessness began to make themselves known among
the audience. Still, it is very likely that the performers
were already experiencing a sort of inner panic, however
little they showed it, long before the Lord Provost, giving a
particularly loud snort and a cry of 'Mine's the big blonde
pair!', turned in his sleep a little too sharply, and fell off his
seat onto the plush carpet below, on which, face-down,
he was fortunately able to continue his slumbers undis-
mayed and unperturbed. Many of the more civic-minded
among the audience flushed with shame at this unlucky
interruption; however, since it was not entirely unexpected, it was all the more easily assimilated and by and
large ignored. For a little longer, the action proceeded as if
nothing untoward had happened. After all, people were
used to this sort of thing by now.

The performers, it should be noticed – the fact was
much appreciated by nearly all concerned – had taken the
trouble to learn the work off by heart, and they were
therefore playing it without any music in front of them.
No scores were in fact in sight, not even for decoration. Of
course, as was also appreciated by some, the fewer free
scores there were drifting hither and yon, the less chance
there was of someone who had no right to do so oppor-
tunistically laying his prying or thieving hands on one of
them. And needless to say, where so much was involved
in the way of prestige and publicity, the experienced
performers had taken great pains to ensure that their
memorisations of the score were flawless. Doubtless they
could have pulled themselves out of any probable lapse by
mere improvisatory technique – but how much better not
to take any such risk! They had rehearsed this piece
almost until it was an ineradicable part of their central

nervous systems. Though to others it was unknown, to them it had been for some while now the piece of music they heard even in their dreams.

However, for all this, the fact was that, probably after ten minutes or so – and certainly before twenty had passed – they both realised that something was going quite seriously amiss. Though they were playing in perfect accord and knew that they must therefore (presumably) still be within the music they had tirelessly rehearsed together for many hours over the preceding week or more, they both knew, or felt they knew, that what they were now playing contained material which was as wholly novel to them as it was to the most virgin-eared listener. Some of it was vaguely familiar to them; but much was completely unknown. And when they both plainly saw, from the ornate new public clock which hung in great splendour at the back of the hall, that it was now distinctly over half an hour since their performance had commenced, they knew beyond all doubt that some serious flaw or anomaly had entered into the circumstances; for never had any of their previous straight-through performances at rehearsal lasted for more than something between twenty-one and twenty-two minutes, however fluid their passing moods might have rendered the agreed tempi. In short, some worryingly unknown or uncanny element had evidently entered right into the fabric of the rejuvenated music. A sort of noble anguish began to seep into their features. As highly-strung artists, of course, they feared that the problem must lie within themselves. And, indeed, to be quite honest, it is not easy to see where else it might comfortably be located.

As for the members of the audience, doubtless they were affected in a wide variety of ways, depending on how much they knew in advance of the dimensions of the piece they were due to hear. There should be noted the further complication that the announced running-order decreed that, after the first performance and a rumour of formal speeches from one or two of the principals involved, proceedings were due to conclude with a repeat performance of the fantasy. This was intended to allow the music due weight – and also to provide all concerned with the satisfaction of knowing that they had been present at both the first and the second public performance of a piece which was virtually sure to become a standard part of the repertory at once. Thus it is possible that some of the audience simply assumed that the speeches had either been rescheduled or (no doubt mercifully) cancelled; that the piece was being performed twice running; and that they had somehow, perhaps through some minor inadvertence, missed the brief interval between the separate renditions. Yet surely, in that case, they would have asked themselves why they had heard no applause? Or might applause perhaps not be quite the thing to do on so solemn and dignified an occasion?

After about an hour or so, however, the first, intrepid leave-taker got up from his seat and, bowed almost double with polite public contrition, made his way as softly and inconspicuously as he could towards the great door. And there it was. This established a precedent which, with ever-increasing momentum, others were not slow to imitate. One or two of them, as if to disclaim responsibility, pursed their lips, ostentatiously consulted their watches, and shook their heads as they left. After an hour and a half, there were already clear patches of empty seats visible in the auditorium. The anguished performers watched each departure with pleading eyes – but all to no avail, whatever their plea was or was for, since the departing figures never once returned their look.

After two hours, even the genuine music-lovers, and those members of the audience who were under the influence of mind-altering drugs, began to suspect that something was amiss. But still the performers played: on and on. Two and a half hours. Still there was no conclusion; no break in the music; no final chords. Always the half-resolution, and then continuance. Three hours. Oh God. Four hours. Sounds of noise and laughter would now be filtering in occasionally from the buffet elsewhere in the building. No-one who had left ever returned to see how things were going on; and no new member of the public or inquisitive representative of any communications medium ever seemed to show very much interest in proceedings. Was it all, somehow, meant? After eight hours, the Lord Provost, still peacefully asleep, was lifted up by concerned staff and ceremoniously carried out of the auditorium. He had another full day ahead of him tomorrow, after all, in his representative capacity. Authority, in the profoundest sense, never sleeps. And at this point, the demented duo very nearly concluded, as if some particularly baleful and responsible agent had been removed from their midst; but there was a moment of hesitation between them, a moment of irresolution, and the chance, it seems, was lost forever.

Eventually, of course, it was time to lock up the hall for the night. The entire audience, but for one man who had had a great deal to do with the provenance of this music, had departed by now. This man was, perhaps I should add, weeping copiously for some reason or other. The performers by now were utterly off in world of their own. Whether a better one or a worse one, who can say? Some things are not for us to know.

Next morning, those who opened the place up could tell that the performance was still underway. The music was still going on. They could hear it; they didn't even need to look. To be quite honest, I am not entirely sure, as yet, whether it has stopped by now or not. Personal enquiry, I'm afraid, has never particularly been my strong point. I heard there was a fire in the building recently, but I didn't bother going to investigate. It may well have happened before the concert. I suppose the fact is I had better things to do. Also, I am not very interested in fires, from whatever motive. Anyway, I'm lazy. I don't seek to deny or disguise or extenuate that no doubt unglorious truth. Even so, I for one would be extremely surprised if the place is not still there. You only have to look at it to know that it has an air of durability about it. And, apart from anything else, the impulse to continue is surely deeply embedded in the logic of music. It's part of the fabric. There is always that consolation.

The Door

He could hardly believe it. There it was at last. The door. Such a small door too, to arrive at after so much searching. Such a small door. Just beside another one. But he knew it would lead to her. He knew she was behind it. At last, after years of searching, he had finally managed to discover where she lived. This was it here.

He walked slowly up to it, still greatly incredulous. So many manoeuvres had been necessary; so much had had to be learned. There had been so many false trails which had for a while deluded him; there had been so much wrong information which had led him astray in the past. All in all, it was astonishing that he had persevered for the ridiculously long time that it had required for him to be successful.

Still finding it almost easier to disbelieve than believe, he reached out and ran his fingertips over the painted wood of the door. This was it. It answered the description utterly. He suddenly felt certain that this was indeed the right door for him. He suddenly knew. At last he had found it. She would be there. Nothing could be more certain.

He raised his hand triumphantly and hammered

175

against the wood. Possibly he used too much force. More probably, the door was waiting to be put right. But anyway, what happened was that the door keeled over and fell on top of him, killing him instantly. It was, it turned out, a very heavy door indeed.

The Next Life

I walked up the corridor, went through the small wooden archway at the top, and turned left, as I had been advised. No-one else was there, but this was no surprise to me. I was expecting that. A sign on the wall said, *'Wait There for Fifteen Minutes'*. I automatically complied with it, needless to say.

When a due period had elapsed, I continued on my way. Perhaps I even left a few seconds before the quarter of an hour was quite up, for there has always been a pronounced streak of healthy rebelliousness in my nature. It has always been there. I don't apologise for it. I suppose, to be honest, I am even quite proud of it.

It was, I found, a fairly complex interior. Often I had to choose whether to go to the right or the left or straight on – which is to say, I would have had to make such choices for myself, presumably with much difficulty, had there not invariably been a sign displayed at eye level, telling me which to choose. And always, at the bottom, in tiny lettering, as if as an afterthought, there was added the warning not to try to turn back. This, of course, made my progress so much easier than it might otherwise have been.

I omit some of the more trivial details. Midway up a stairway, I was rather puzzled by a sign which told me to eat the food I had brought with me. What? I had brought no food with me. I had not been advised that this would be necessary. How to cope with this unexpected challenge? I hesitated for a while until what I rather believe was something of an inspiration struck me. I decided to compromise, by merely pretending to be eating some food for a few seconds, before continuing on my way. So, for a brief while, I went through the motions of mastication while otherwise stationary, and then departed. I confess to feeling rather pleased with myself at this point. I was sure that this would be thought to be a very wise and mature response on my part, if anyone should ever get to hear of it. That, it seemed to me, was the difficulty about all of it. When would anyone ever get to hear of it?

At the top of what seemed to me be an important stairway the corridor led off both to left and right. But directly in front there was only a large window. I at once discounted that possibility; although time has not convinced me that I was necessarily right in so doing. I was entirely unable to find any indication of which way I was supposed to choose to race down. I waited for a long while to see whether or not anyone would turn up to advise me, but no-one did. I was not on my own, of course; still, there was no-one else there. In the end, after a considerable period of anguish, I decided that it must be meant that I should make the decision for myself. This was an extremely fraught moment. As I happened to be nearer to the left side of the top of the stairway, I chose to turn left. Still, I must admit I was not at first very pleased by such a way of doing things.

Even so, all seemed to go well for a while thereafter. However, eventually, after a few unimportant interludes, I found myself standing by a doorway, confronted by a sign which told me to confess all I felt I was afraid of. I walked on past this without going in. After all, one cannot spend one's whole posthumous life responding to threats. Soon I found myself faced with an alcove which bore a sign telling me to confess, even if only to myself, those aspects of my attitude to existence which I somehow deep down knew to be in some way tinged with dishonesty. I read it twice. That is definitely what it said.

This, I felt, was enough. I had not come here to be insulted or played with. I turned back instantly and tried to retrace my steps. At first, I seemed to wander about uncertainly for a considerable time. Then, much later, when I was passing (not, I think, for the first time) an inviting chair in one of the remote side corridors, I decided just to sit right down and wait right there, without further ado, in peace and comfort at last. I felt that, by now, I at least deserved that much. It was surely very little to ask of anyone. Or, indeed, of no-one. I felt I had done all I could reasonably be expected to do, and that now it was up to others to proceed, whether with me or without me, as best they could. No doubt we all reach that point at some time or other.

I began to suspect that it would have been much better for me to have chosen to go in the other direction when I had had the chance, or in some other direction anyway; but I knew it was far too late to do anything of any great significance about that. Anyway, whatever one chooses, one has to leave something out. So I remain here instead. I have no intention whatever of moving. I shall stay here for as long as it takes. Or until I see someone else. Or something like that. I am absolutely adamant about that. I am not going to move. I have done enough. Let someone else do some work from here on in. I am perfectly prepared to wait.

The Philosophy of the Wardrobe

As the old lady was walking past the tall wardrobe in her hallway – which had been one of the proudest possessions of the family for well over a century – it toppled over and fell onto her, moved by who knows what freak. The severity of her plight may easily be imagined. No-one heard it happen. One might say, surely at least the old lady herself heard it, but the fact is that she is profoundly deaf; quite apart from the fact that she is at the moment also unconscious, and perhaps even dead. Some would even dare to claim that, if no-one heard a noise, there can have been no noise – for what is noise if it is not something that is heard? What sort of thing is an unheard noise? Are we to say that it is something which would be heard if someone who could hear things were near enough to the event or process to pick up the appropriate vibrations? To which I think the answer must be, quite simply, Yes.

Or are we advised to suppose that, since no-one heard the wardrobe topple over, therefore it toppled over silently – and that the old lady thus would not have heard it even if she had not been entirely devoid of all such aural capacity? But does she not even have a hearing-aid? My

181

feeling is that she does. Is she wearing it? Have the batteries perhaps run down to utter exhaustion? There is, very probably, a fruitful area of doubt and ambiguity here; a complex tangle of possibilities which is surely well worth investigating. Is it even supposed to occur to us, perhaps, that the wardrobe in fact cannot have fallen at all – for if it had fallen, there would have been a sound associated with this event, but there was no sound (for no sound was heard), and therefore there can have been no toppling wardrobe? This, however, I suggest, does not carry very much conviction. Particularly not to the old lady. If she is conscious, that is to say.

Be that as it may, it does make one rather wonder what all the neighbours were doing at the time. Everyone was evidently elsewhere. There are certainly other domiciles in the area in which the sound of the tragedy would have been clearly received, had there been anyone present there with normal aural capacities. Indeed, at the other end of the street, another old woman with just as nice a bust (although that is, of course, almost entirely irrelevant) has also just had a fainting fit. I say, 'other old woman', but the fact is that since I feel it is my duty to minimise human suffering, I should perhaps point out that the earlier old lady in fact turned into a frog just before the accident with her cupboard. Unfortunate for the frogs, perhaps, but there we are. In this world we can very rarely be entirely free of loss. I saw a frog once, you know. It was sitting in the middle of a normally busy road at midnight, looking perfectly relaxed. A charming sight, all in all.

So there we are. The second old lady (or old man, if you prefer, since no-one but a gross pervert, if I may be allowed that term, particularly wants females to suffer) has clutched at her own tall wooden wardrobe in the

182

attempt to steady herself – also, very possibly, a source of some family pride – with the result that she has pulled that wardrobe down on top of herself, thereby rendering herself also unconscious. A curious coincidence, if coincidence it is. Are coincidences possible? If not, what is? Has the second of these phenomena directly resulted from the first? After all, it did follow it, which is something. Few, surely, would like to claim that the first phenomenon resulted from the second. Well, perhaps some advanced cosmic physicists might like to, but fortunately very few people can ever understand what it is they are talking about. However, the thing I always like to say is this: that the most important task facing the thinker is the responsibility to take reality seriously. This is quite true. Whatever we go on to, it is from that point that we must proceed. I would like to develop the point further, but all that must wait until I have hastened to the nearest telephone, wherever it is exactly, and have called for the ambulance and alerted the emergency services. After all, even writers have their duties as citizens, have they not? Indeed they do. They do indeed. I have never denied that for a moment.

The Special Messenger

Whereat the angel, a little confused after his journey, moved about the room for a while, picking up and examining things, and putting them back approximately where he had found them, with a bemused expression on his visage. Sometimes, also, he would bump lightly off the walls. Evidently he was still not quite habituated to his new surroundings. This he did for rather a long while, until the young lady, becoming somewhat impatient, asked him: 'So. Who did you say you were, and why were you sent here?'

'My name is Khlunt,' he replied, 'I think. As I have already told you more than once. Six times in fact. One – two – five – eight – three – six. Yes. Six times. I have come to bring you astonishing tidings from a dimension which is ontologically entirely disjunct from your own. Why won't you listen to me?'

'But I am listening!' cried the maiden. 'Just look at how wide open my appropriate appendages are! What tidings are they which you wish to bring?' asked the tender virgin, her curiosity once again piqued. 'Why don't you just tell me them in simpler terms?'

'It is so difficult to put it in terms which entities so

limited as you small-brained earth-people are will under-stand,' he said, with rather offensive hauteur, as he tripped over a small stool and fell into the fire – from which he quickly re-emerged, his lips pursed in irritation. 'Or do I mean, "small-breasted"? Why am I expected to remember so many tedious details?'

'That rather depends,' she said sadly.

'Actually, to be quite honest,' he continued, 'I may as well come clean here. The fact is, I have entirely forgotten the reason I was sent here. Gone, gone, gone. This sort of thing is bound to happen sometimes. I'm not infinite, after all. The message has simply gone and slipped my mind – what's so strange about that? These things hap-pen. I have had a lot to contend with recently. Excuse me a moment, will you? I know what I'll do. I'll just nip back home and get things sorted out in an absolute jiffy. Five seconds. And I'll be back here on your planet Theare in next to no time at all, you just see if I'm not. One moment please.'

Saying which, with a smile, he disappeared into thin air. She knew perfectly well she would never see him again. It had sounded like a very obvious excuse. And she was right. No-one ever saw him again. Possibly it was not very important after all. That is surely the likeliest ex-planation.

Fallen off the Edge

Here we are. The last summer before the great war, perhaps. All over the place, artists are sketching fruit and flowers and the insides and outsides of innumerable windows, mostly very badly though the particular building is usually adequate at least; and many views of different lanes, and people travelling on various stretches of water, and women wearing an incredibly wide variety of often noticeably wide hats. I could go on for just about forever with this; and this is very likely what many of them thought too, or perhaps they merely assumed it. It is what people tend to assume. Why should it change? It has been like this forever so far. Apart from anything else, the death of someone puts him into an untypical state. The same goes for her.

They stop every so often; or they go on every so often. Look. A gentleman in an office is writing an ordinary letter. In many woods people are walking while in conversation; or they are breathing in the fine air alone, rejoicing in it or wondering how to continue. We say nothing of the perverts, of course. And in one or two of the perhaps more oblique or tangential forests, a man is practising with a revolver, trying to increase his proficiency on the instrument. It would be wrong to think that none of this will lead to anything. Everything must presumably lead to something, and some things lead immediately to astonishment.

Mrs Farquharson, for instance, has just committed an act of gross indecency in West Regent Street with a chartered accountant. She has a sudden intense conviction that her life will never be the same again, and perhaps that it will not be improved by recent events. She doubts whether it will be ruined by it. The same is possibly true of many of those who will play a less than central role in the upcoming broad tragedy. We walk past the scenes of their lives, talking about things which consume our interest, after nearly a further century has passed. Yet, even so, at that time all over the continent, newspapers are being raised and lowered. A vast rustling beyond the insults. I mean, beyond the insects. They are drinking tea. They are drinking coffee. They are drinking milk. They are drinking water. Some are even drinking poisons, I suppose; or disgusting fluids which I shall not further mention. Or perhaps they are having a word about the condition of the world. They are saying, Surely you do not intend to go out like that? They are saying: Why do you not speak to me? By and large, they probably do not feel that it is too bad. By and large we don't.

It is fairly normal for something to look as if it is going to go on like this forever. Stay a little longer if you like. Oh, there's plenty of time yet. Lift up the same paper; watch an atmospheric effect; put down a different one. Much the same goes for dresses, I suppose. Virtually all over the continent. A little sense; much nonsense. Nothing very significant will ever come of it, don't you worry. Tell me what you have been doing since last I saw you. Not everything, obviously. The highlights are all I want. And so it continues. Until.

The Usual Victim

I remember once reading out from a book of mine at a pleasant and sophisticated literary gathering, or some such unlikely occurrence, a passage which contained the rather offhand remark that the birth of religion was also the birth of surrealism. This perhaps somewhat over-simplified observation led to a certain mild amount of friction in discussions afterwards – although since the word *surrealism* is a mere straightforward domestication of the French word for 'super-realism', and since religion claims to be dealing with things that lie beyond mere surface reality, things above reality, behind reality, beside reality and so forth, super-real things, things *in another dimension* (precise meaning, unknown), there should at least be surely a sort of verbal appropriateness in the remark, however unprofound and deaf to all that is rare and fine in our existence here below in the actual universe it might be.

Very well. But what, then, of this picture that I have before me of a monk kneeling in an attractively varied landscape? A companion of his seems to have dozed off at his side. Distant crowds to his left and right presumably indicate other episodes in his life, in the intriguing and

191

almost filmic fashion of the time. This is evidently the very *bonhomme* after whom I was named, the one and only Francis of Assisi, who lived in the real world, one might say, somewhat slantingly.

It would be little more than a highly attractive if somewhat conventional image of figures in landscape, done by an old master whose very name has not survived – he seems to have worked in Cologne in the years fore and aft of 1500 – were it not for a feature which is astonishing enough even in the smallish black and white reproduction which is all I have to go on.

Which is? I shall tell you. After all, the whole thing would be rather pointless if I didn't. The fact is that, away up in the sky, almost at the extremest edge of the picture, there is a large, winged crucifix flying through the air. In fact, it rather looks to have two sets of wings – bird-like, or angel-like, feathery wings. Not that a flying crucifix with four wings – or with only one, for that matter – looks very much odder, if at all, than a flying crucifix that has only two of them. One does rather find oneself wondering just how it managed to take off and land, but doubtless that is a narrowly literalist and appallingly *unimaginative* objection. We are not actually meant to ask real questions about such sublime matters, are we? God forbid. Let us approach with condign humility those matters (in other words, spiritual matters) which are more important than mere reality, that state of affairs which is altogether too terribly limited to offer us the sustenance which our deepest urges require. And so on.

There is, of course, a body on the crucifix – and it is the usual victim. And five lines, looking exactly like ropes, are extended from various parts of his body, soaring vastly down through the air, rather like the cables you might find in some admirable modern bridges. They match up

192

with the corresponding parts of the body of the kneeling monk. They are where the body of Christ, as far as I remember, is supposed to have seeped blood during his final passion. Which is to say, while he was dying. A slow death that man has died indeed. Both feet; both palms – where the nails were driven in: although I believe it is nowadays widely agreed that the Romans in their cruci- fixions did not drive nails through the palms, which would simply not have been able to bear the full weight of a body without quickly tearing right through – and then a final mark in the side, where the dead charismatic insurrectionist's corpse – if such it was; and it probably was – was pierced by an unimpressed and officious man in uniform, according to some or other of those highly inventive merchants of anecdote and legend who are sanctified by the term, gospel-writers. Only one of the four evangelists has this detail, I think. Obviously it had not been remembered in time for the others to use it. Fortunately, some people have better memories than others, even if they are slower working.

The stigmata, in other words. Similar seepages, by a process which is, to say the least, metabolically somewhat obscure, are being sympathetically induced in the body of the monk by the corpse on the swooping cross. (I say 'corpse' since I understand it is only Muslims who nowa- days believe the man did not actually die.) But for the moment it looks almost as if the high crucifix is a kite which the saint is flying. It is attached to him by ropes. How is he to break free? How is *it* to break free? To what use will he turn this mysterious and non-functional bleeding? If this visual story had not existed, it would have taken someone of the calibre of Max Ernst or René Magritte to have invented it. Some surrealist has been at work here anyway.

More like Ernst than Magritte, actually. Magritte's pictures are quite often pure exercises in logic, if you know how to look at them. And an exercise in logic is clearly something remote from this enterprise of the Meister von St. Severin.

Of course, there is more to life than logic. There is more than logic to everything but logic, after all. However, there is not more to life than life. Absolutely everything surely ought to be enough?

As a straightforward and fairly self-evident footnote we may as well draw the simple and obvious conclusion that all stigmatics, however revered, are actually frauds of one sort or another – usually conscious and deliberate ones, I dare say. Of course, there may also be some who have so lost sight of the real world and what they are actually doing in it that they have managed to delude themselves before or while deluding other people too.

A harsh-sounding verdict, perhaps, but at least it posits a mechanism the existence of which virtually everybody accepts. We all know that fraud occurs in this life. As the alternative explanation is not really an explanation at all – merely a noun (stigmatism) hiding behind a label (mystery – a reverential way of indicating, and indeed of rather boasting about, a total systematic ignorance of what is supposed to be going on) – the judgement of any serious and honest moral being has to favour the only actual explanation which is on offer here. Which is to say, fraud. Thank you. Truth is under no compulsion to be complex. Well: how could it be?

The Absolute End

At first there was nothing to it. It was just an ordinary lazy warm summery day by the seashore at Lairgs. A large crowd strolled about, enjoying the warmth and the scenery and the many attractions on offer, some of which were none too easy to find. Others played on the pebbly beach; or they reclined in the broad expanse of warm sand which curved towards the so-called Chinese Pavilion. Or they admired each other's buttocks in a mature and responsible manner in the thick local foliage. It was about two o'clock in the afternoon; perhaps slightly later. But it was certainly not yet half past. I am quite sure of that. The clock on the steeple was unable to get that far.

No-one was counting the waves, of course. Certainly not all of them. That would be a rather futile occupation, I think most people would agree, even a complete mistake such as yourself – though, of course, the question of how God manages to spend his time is such a fraught topic that many have decided it is safer just to say that he is beyond time, or outside time. How exactly he spends his time there – or inexactly, for that matter – is, it is felt, a question which one cannot reasonably ask. Still, one would rather like to know. No? Oh well. Perhaps not.

It is always so vulgar, when people ask questions that one simply cannot answer, not realising that the fault lies within themselves.

Anyway, the waves were indifferently bustling in and drifting out, as usual, when one of them, of no obvious distinction otherwise, certainly not taller or faster or anything like that, simply continued to advance through the previous peak of their approach. It speedily covered the beach, climbed the wall, sped through the carpark, crossed the road, and almost before people could quite grasp what was happening, if they ever did, it had taken over the whole town and had mastered the hinterland beyond. And that was that.

Within an hour or so, it had covered the whole of Europe, and within an hour and a half it, or what it had produced or led to, had covered the entire earth. The effect would seem therefore to have been somewhat cumulative in its execution. Scientists would have been fascinated, obviously, if they hadn't all been wiped out. But they were. Nature, or whatever you want to call it, had done it. Commentary was futile.

As to why I and those who are dear to me were spared among this universal inundation – I have given this a lot of thought, naturally enough I dare say under the circumstances, and there remains a certain amount of doubt in my mind. I can only suppose, doing the best I can, that it is because the numerous orifices of my wife are so nearly perfect that they can serve as an adequate model – from nothing, as it were – of absolutely everything that might be of any importance. Unless perhaps it is her face that is doing it. As for me, I suppose I am their official admirer or chronicler or nurturer or something like that. Certainly, it is true that after one has kissed her various existential parts it becomes more or less impossible to take art or philosophy very seriously – although, of course, one tries one's best. What else can one do with them, after all?

As for what yet remains to be done, I suppose that is simple enough. Having, somehow or other, hardly through our own sole efforts, found that which lies beyond actual reality – which is to say, God – we must now bravely seek for that which lies beyond God. For that which is, by definition, more important than even the most important. For the summit beyond or above the peak. The dimension beyond the 'final' dimension. The vision beyond mere vision. The limit beyond the limit. The goal beyond the goal. The life beyond life. In fact, the more or less any term you care for beyond the previous stage of whichever term this might be, if anything. That one cannot put a clear signification to any of this is perhaps slightly unfortunate, but, of course, it is hardly the salient point. The vital point is to bedazzle yourself into supposing that you are doing it. For if you are doing it then, obviously, it must be possible.

Of course, this is something which it is difficult – nay, probably in fact impossible – for our limited finite human minds to grasp. That must be honestly acknowledged. We are indeed limited and finite. Or, in other words, real. Nonetheless, we must do the best we can, even if in the attempt we form phrases and expressions which to the smug and the unsympathetic and those who fetishise mere accuracy, pedantry, truth, honesty, correspondence with what actually in all its limitations exists and so forth do not convey any clear meaning at all. Which sound like, not to say are identical to, absolute rubbish, in fact. But what can we reasonably be expected to do about that? It is not us who made the world after all, is it? Is it?

For how may one expect the greatest and most supreme meaning of all, the meaning which lies beyond all

197

meaning, and beyond that too, and so on forever, to be at all capturable in the limping language of creatures so limited as ourselves, who have ideas such as these? Speech can create God but it cannot approach him. God, said Pontius Plotinus, the well-known ancient seer and drug addict, is not essence, but beyond essence. Not the essence of everything. To call him that is to claim too little. He is Everything; He is that which underpins Everything; and He is also that which lies beyond this Everything, both of them, too. Of course he is. How could he be anything else, whatever this actually is? And then he is whatever may be behind that too. And so on again for as long as you like, until perhaps you have managed to hypnotise yourself to sleep.

After all, if religion teaches us anything, and it is not entirely clear that it does, it teaches us the immense, nay the infinite value of renouncing what exists for what does not. We must, now that we realise this, in turn strike out for that which is beyond that which is beyond essence and existence. And so on. One would not be enough. It is impossible, perhaps; and it does not make sense anyway; but surely it is not the human condition, for our questing and never quite satisfied spirits merely to accept that the world is what it is and try to do with this whatever good we can? Can you be serious? I mean to say, that would so easy; so humiliating; so limiting; so muddily *realistic* – would it not? We are, in short, made for better things than mere reality. Half a bridge is better than none. Thoughts that are nowhere are better than our own. Since I have conclusively proved this, there is no more that I need to say just at the moment.

The Witness

It was obvious by now that I had got lost, in the sense that I did not know *exactly* where I was. However, I did retain a keen general awareness of the broad layout of the city beyond. I was fairly sure of where the river was; and the main temple; and the station, and so forth. That should be as much as I needed. If I kept moving in any single direction through the confusing warren of the Old Town, I was fairly certain I would soon enough stumble out upon one of the broader boulevards; after which it was merely a question of choosing the right direction, and the middle-distance skyline would surely be of decisive help to me here. One would rather never be lost, I dare say; still, this, I thought, should not turn out to be a particularly worrying episode. One could not stray far.

Unfortunately, every so often I had to make totally blind choices to go right or left when the road ended; and after a while I could not but believe that I must be retracing my steps and repeating myself to a certain extent, for otherwise I would surely have already emerged from the narrow old streets and lanes, which could hardly be so extensive as to keep me for such a long time if I had been following some direct route through them. Of course the thoroughfares looked virtually indistinguishable to me anyway. The passers-by were regarding me, as a further complication, with what seemed to me by and large to be a very obvious lack of enthusiasm. My foreignness evidently stood out far more than I had thought it would. Perhaps they were less used to strangers in this more than somewhat forbidding and self-contained district – and as for a recurring stranger! What could that be but either a threat or an unexpected opportunity? I tried not to spend too much time on the question: an opportunity for what?

On an inspiration I had slipped down a nondescript little stairway, and I saw to my great relief that the street I had descended into was slightly broader than most of the others – which suggested to me that salvation was near, and that with a bit of luck it must eventually debouch into an even more important thoroughfare. Some playing children looked up from their unintelligible and complex game and laughed at me, presumably from mere joie de vivre. I smiled back at them, unconvincingly I fear, and then proceeded on my way with a slight increase of speed. The last thing I wanted was to become the set focus of anyone's attention. To my disappointment, the road ahead took a quick dogleg and became narrow again; however I had no choice but to follow it onwards anyway. I was certainly not going to turn round and go back.

A couple of people were standing at a doorway up ahead. They seemed very excited by something. I could hear that shouting was going on inside the house at which they were standing. They were gesticulating and talking volubly with some of the inmates, and were breaking aside to make strange ululating cries of what I now suppose must have been triumph; although at the time I think I was dismayed at the thought that they might be fear – that something was happening which was frightening them. In which case, would I simply be allowed to pass unhindered; might my help not in some way be sought? Or might it even be anger at something or other which caused those strange calls?

As I came nearer, I began to make out some of the exclamations and cries. My command of the local language is of course far from perfect; nonetheless I am confident that it is accomplished enough for me to be able to interpret a simple sentence when I hear one. Particularly a sentence – or, rather, a group of them – which is grammatically as simple as, 'God has just been born here. He has just been born here. Our God is here. We are saved once again.' Of course, I missed much else. However, one of the men noticed me passing, and he shouted out to me in the excess of his joy, 'Stranger, you are passing at a moment when the new time has begun.' Something like that. Then he turned to his companion and said, 'Look! A complete and probably lost stranger goes by. Just like it was said would happen so long ago. Here it is. It has happened exactly as was foretold.' Then there followed further cries and exclamations and shrieks, but I was only too pleased to have been able to make my way round the next corner without getting roped into things any further. I was on tenterhooks lest I should hear someone following me at speed, eager to draw me back into their unprecedented delirium. A few minutes later, I at last got out onto a road I recognised. From here the way back to my hotel was simpler than I could reasonably have hoped for, and it required merely another ten minutes or so on foot. Whew! That was close! Needless to say, for the rest of the day I deliberately stayed indoors, recovering from what I still think might well have been a very near thing indeed. Such, at least, is how it seemed to me.

Timbuktu

As usual I had gone the last few minutes on foot. It was a beautiful morning. It was one of those mornings so beautiful that you thought, fair enough, this is it: after all its past experiments the weather, or the world in general, has at last got it exactly right. It can stop now. This is it. It has knocked it off finally. Anything else will just spoil it. It can do every morning like this in future and no-one in their right mind will ever complain. And then the next day arrives, of course, miserable and pouring. Or just miserable. Or not quite as right anyway, that is the main thing.

Anyway, I had to stand waiting for a break in the traffic or a change in the lights. Any cosmopolitan sophisticate will instantly understand what I mean. Across the road was the door I would soon have to go in through. I might already have been going through it, just like that man there, whoever he was, right now; exactly at this moment – if I had been hurrying earlier on. Who could that man be, just as a matter of interest? Didn't he look rather like a plain-clothes policeman? No. That's not of prime importance. He's someone else – that's the point. Mind you, he always is, isn't he? My feeling is he probably smells a bit too. But perhaps I am being unfair. You can't always tell just by looking.

But why hurry? Everything was just too right. How could any change be an improvement on this? I dare say it could be, in theory, since I didn't have a meter on me to gauge levels of contentment. Damn and blast, I had left my newly patented Contentmentometer at home again! And even if I had had one I couldn't guarantee that it would have been giving a maximum reading. How could I have done that? No-one could have done that. It might not even have had a maximum point marked on it. A hundred; a thousand; and suchlike. Or perhaps even, One. No. It would have had to be infinite; open-ended. No top at all. Topless, in fact. Maybe that was why they hadn't been designed or manufactured in the first place. There would be a market for these machines, certainly; the only problem was that they could not be made. They were not feasible as a manufacturing proposition. That was the one thing preventing it. The only drawback was its fundamental impossibility. Everything else was ready and in place. But you can't get near infinity, as the kiddies try to learn, and the advanced minds tend to forget.

What was I saying? As if I didn't know. After all, I can read as well as you, can't I? Certainly I can. Or perhaps even better, whatever you might think. Many will find that arrogance grossly unappealing, you know. So. Enough of that. What was I saying? I would already have been inside the building, actually inside the building, inside the actual building, not outside it like I still was now, but, on the contrary, inside it, if I hadn't decided to – but now I have to cross. Sorry. Now or never. I have to cross the road. I yielded to the temptation, and that is that. Well, I wasn't being forced across at gunpoint, obviously. So few of us ever are, really. And I can't just stand there forever, or even for just the rest of my life, however pleasant it is. You can't just stand in places, however innocently, enjoying what it feels like to be just standing there with the air and the light on you, and the people passing you on either side in both directions, and even the traffic-sound right for a change. Hello, sexy. It would be an obstruction in their path, for one thing. You would be labelled an eccentric, and dragged out of the road by responsibly elected officials. A crowd might even gather to applaud. What sexual organs they all are sometimes, eh? Ugly ones too, I mean.

You have to cross with them. That's all there is to it. Cross. Go across. You have to. That's the right thing to do. Don't shit yourself, as some of the others may be doing; just walk across the, at present, comparatively inactive road. But this is perfect, here this, waiting to walk, waiting, walking; why should I want to change it? I don't. Why should I want to actually arrive at my destination? I don't; I've already said that. I'll say it again. It is a dubious achievement on most days, as I think it was Aristotle who pointed out somewhere, and a scandalous anti-climax on a morning like this. After all, he seems to have pointed out most things. But did it make him happy, that is what I sometimes wonder. However, I had to move, Aristotle or no Aristotle.

I'll just go past the door and take a turn round the block. I have four minutes. I wonder if that'll be enough. Four minutes and ten seconds if the watch is exactly accurate, which it obviously isn't. I might even be late already, I suppose. I have been coming to this place for over two years, but I don't think I have ever circumnavigated this particular block of buildings. Why should I, after all? Usually you arrive here as directly as possible, and you leave it to get somewhere else as soon as you can. Besides which, I lack an ocean-going vessel. It is a striking part of modern life I always think, how rarely people ever actually walk all the way round a building or a block of buildings. Or did I read that somewhere old and tedious? Kafka? Proust, possibly. I remember nearly reading a book of his years ago. Certainly one of them. Rather vague, I thought. But perhaps I should give him another try some time.

Right. So why am I going in through the door anyway? I don't want to do this. I really don't want to do this. I should have kept walking. I can understand other people not preferring my own preferences, but why do I always keep doing the same thing myself? Why can't I always prefer my own preferences? Maybe someone is standing outside that tobacconist's, or that travel agent's more likely, though I don't think it'll have opened yet, or in just such a position that you don't know which shop she is nearer to; and she's looking round for help. Yes, that would be me beside you, if I had only kept moving in a straight line. She is seeking help. It could have been from me. A heaven-sent opportunity!

And look! What a face! It's the face! It does exist! It's that face at last – the one you always knew you would recognise at once as soon as you saw it. And you worried if you *really* would, and here it is – and you have. You have. It's the right face without a doubt. Cretin! (For thus I occasionally address myself, when under almost unbearable distress.) She is looking round for help. She is looking round for help – she wants to know the way to the nearest religious meeting-point, for instance – and whoever she gets help from, it'll not be from you! You've missed your chance, the one great chance of your life, and you had to go in to work just like it was any other day! You had to change your mind about walking needlessly round the building you work inside. Tragedy. Cata-strophe. It is all so typical.

Mind you: why does she want to get to a religious meeting-point at this time in the morning, for heaven's sake? Is this perhaps a frisson of weirdness? Not that that matters as such. Whatever she wants. Her happiness, that's the important thing. Be as weird as you like. Do whatever you want, my darling. Believe whatever crap you like, if it makes your little heart beat calmly. Just don't go talking to strange men, dearest, that's all. If I may call you that. One has one's ambitions. And where am I? No use at all. I am not there at just the right moment. I'm in that building that she can see just behind her if she turns round, but what good is that going to do anybody? Don't bother; don't bother. Don't turn round. I might as well be in Timbuktu. It isn't worth it. Not now. Being that close just isn't good enough. You might as well have stayed at home in bed. Don't turn round. You deserve better than a halfwit like that. In fact, from your point of view it was probably a lucky escape. Good. On you go and talk to someone else. I certainly don't deserve it, that's for sure; and the window I work at faces another street anyway. I might as well be in Timbuktu. Possibly I am. That would explain a lot. Or a little. Or nothing. What does it matter? That's odd. I wonder why that man is standing on the top of that tall stationary vehicle. Let him. I don't suppose it's very important, actually.

Some Magnificent Achievements

A pure land, apparently untouched for many miles. Cold water; cold earth. But it is not yet the worst of the weather. The wind flickers and dies yet again. It seems unassailably empty. Another hour passes. Another year. Another month. Another hour. Another two minutes. Then, at just this moment, a boatful of intrepid men land. Crying out joyously, they point to left and right. If it is an island, it must be an enormous island. Screams of exhilaration and achievement. Various bizarre objects are set up. They fall to their knees. Soon they gloriously concelebrate a ritual which purports to remember the actions, wildly inaccurately, of a man who died very many centuries ago, over a continent and an ocean away, in the attempt to save a tribe which they by no means belong to. They eat what is supposed to be his flesh. They commemorate various events which never in fact happened, though it would probably be an instantly fatal mistake to attempt to point this out just at the moment. The truth has its place, and that is not here.

In the distance, unobserved by them, a cautiously passing native observes a strange vehicle, a strange group of strangely dressed strangers, doing something profoundly strange. After a few minutes, in disbelief, he hurries off. An emergency meeting is formed. One group speaks for welcome and brotherhood. For friendship. For sharing the earth. For trusting these strange emissaries who have doubtless come to do some good before going away again to wherever it is they came from. Somewhere over there. Over the sea. In the blessed lands. The other group speaks for enmity, constructive pessimism and naked force. This second group is triumphant. They move swiftly. They surround the strangers just as they are raising their voices in joy at the end of the celebration of their safe arrival. A flurry of arrows. Sharp metallic edges. Most of the newcomers are killed. A few still run. They are hacked down. The natives retire. Silence. Victory. Beyond the river, inaudible here, they cry out praises to the great God Hlomquon, who has once again led them to victory. They dance their dances. The cold water continues to lap against the rock. The earth is perhaps slightly richer, thanks to a modest infusion of fresh blood. Or perhaps not. A narrow escape indeed. The first encounter can so often be crucial.

A Brief Vision

A nd in the evening people started emerging from the loch. There were long stretches of water broken by a single figure; there were occasional bursts as a small crowd emerged together and made for the shore. And among them there came out apparently useless little boys, and there came out great strong manly sages, who had been known for miles around for the depth of their wisdom and goodness. And there came out very many people altogether, for however long they had been there, in their many separate entrances. And they did not gather on the cold strand, but spread onwards into the cold hills.

And there came out those who were claimed; and those who were unclaimed. And those who were familiar; and those who were unfamiliar. And those who were about to be loved; and those who were not about to be loved. And there came out all sorts of people. And they dispersed as best they could, and they did what they could do. For what else were they to do?

And at the end of it all, towards nightfall, there drove out a small white car, which turned onto the road at the bank, and travelled back to the city which it had left, earlier that day, in the morning, from its parking-space on a very high bridge which I have already walked over many thousands of times, and no doubt with many others beside me. And it travelled slowly down the west coast, through one small village after another. And at one point it passed the scene of an accident – two smashed cars now empty and pulled some way apart from each other. And it drove on. And it was, as many would try to tell you, an utterly ordinary day.

Yes

We sat together on a public bench in the afternoon sunlight. Other people walked by. We exchanged some fairly trivial words, for by colossal good luck we both spoke the same language. As, I suppose, now I come to think of it, did most of the people who were walking past, whoever they were, those poor but precious superfluities. We were even together at almost the same point in the development of the language. Not that I wish to suggest that anyone had ever used that language to do anything much more worth doing. Certainly not. Even *King Lear* after all is only a play. Mind you. I suppose it could also be said that life is only life. All things are only all things. But then, what else could they be?

A river had flowed between us in our childhood. It was still nearby. Day after day of going to different schools – well, one of mine was a boys' school; there were rules; she would never have got in no matter how hard she had tried. Though I have reason to suspect that she never actually tried at all. Not in the least. And it would not really have been her yet, in a sense, would it? Nor would I have been I yet. I am I, true; but changes of age are also changes of age.

Day after day of that; and morning after morning of more water flowing through between us, carrying all sort of dead and unnecessary matter, I dare say. People. Boats. Excitement, no doubt. And I was ill sometimes; and she was ill sometimes. And I was being shouted at sometimes, no doubt deservedly; and she was being shouted at sometimes. And I was made much of sometimes; and she was made much of sometimes. But never enough, surely. Surely never enough. Or perhaps it was enough, for look what an incomparable effect it had.

And this bench would no doubt already have been here. And on various mornings, certainly on various days, all sorts of people would have been sitting on it; not to mention lying on it. Let me limit the explicit possibilities to those, thank you. Did I even sit on it myself in those days? Perhaps she did too, but it is not her side of the river, and I shall not ask, for I am happier with my assumption that this is the first time she has been here after decades of days when, but for a few dozen, she could always have got here within an hour, if appropriate transport had been provided. But it so rarely is, isn't it? Still, appropriate transport was provided today, and for it to happen even once seems more than one could reasonably have expected.

Some Life

And up every morning past that squat, brooding, dreadful church. What on earth is ever going on inside there? You could easily hide an army in there, but is there ever actually *anybody* inside there? I suppose the man himself must be in there somewhere, perhaps in one of those back rooms, behind one of those strange little ordinary windows you can never quite make sense of. There could be a dozen of them, for all I know. Perhaps he is seducing a parishioner. Perhaps he is thinking about God. Perhaps he is just putting in the day rather like the rest of us. Come to think of it – what am I doing?

That is a good question. Usually I try to avoid questions like that. I am walking past the church, obviously. I am not the person in that shop over there. I am not just at the moment getting into my car. Nor anyone else's car. Nor am I getting out of them. The possibilities are endless. Virtually endless. I am not the person, if any there be, up there behind that bright-red curtain. Evidently colour-blind; or perhaps a connoisseur of something or other. Or perhaps, how do I know it is not the case, it's an object of great sentimental value, that curtain up there, not to say, of *overwhelming* sentimental value.

215

It's the one thing I can't live without. Perhaps it is the only thing that still remains of forty years of almost unbroken happiness? Well, thirty-five at least. Or might it have been handed on with a spasm of hidden relief by a neighbour who couldn't stand the sight of it? Or for a moment longer? Really, why couldn't it just be a nondescript colour like that one right below it, and slightly to the left, and so save you and everyone else all the trouble and bother of these irresolvable but please don't call them barren speculations.

Of course, you could always just go right on up there and ask. A knock at the door. Or a ring at the bell, of course. You go and answer it. Surely it's not the police, or another religious maniac. No. No, it's some mildly scary-looking personage who you may have seen out on a street nearby once or twice, not that you need to have done, asking you about the provenance and significance of your curtains. What could be more normal. What could be more reasonable. Authenticity at last! Come in, come in; I have been longing to tell some sympathetic stranger the truth about them. So there you are: invited in. In you go then, look round in bafflement, commit a murder perhaps, nip back out again, spend the money on a spree which is perhaps to some degree motivated by the desire to hide even from your own conscious mind the lurid and distressing details of the atrocity you have just committed, and never get caught. Never get caught. Very fortunate, see. No stains to talk about. Strangulation, perhaps. Fright. How should I know? How should anyone know? No-one happened to see you at the time. Well, why should they pay you any attention? So – out you go, down by the church – maybe even *into* the church. The main door right in front of it is open, after all. Great. Unburden your soul to a passing, compassionate ecclesiastic. What better? Make full use of the available resources. Steal a candlestick. Then out into the continuing sunlight of morning. What a life! I'm glad I decided to get up this morning after all. Who wouldn't be, under circumstances like this?